The Ric-A-Dam-Doo

Also by DAVID J. BERCUSON

The Fighting Canadians: Canada's Regimental History from New France to Afghanistan, 2008
The Secret Army, 2005
Blood on the Hills: The Canadian Army in the Korean War, 2002
The Patricias: The Proud History of a Fighting Regiment, 2001
Significant Incident: Canada's Army, the Airborne, and the Murder in Somalia, 1996
Battalion of Heroes: The Calgary Highlanders in World War II, 1995
Maple Leaf Against the Axis: Canada's Second World War, 1995
True Patriot: The Life of Brooke Claxton, 1993
Confrontation at Winnipeg: Labour, Industrial Relations and the General Strike, 1990
Canada and the Birth of Israel: A Study in Canadian Foreign Policy, 1985
Reappraising Canadian History, 1982
Fools and Wise Men: The Rise and Fall of the One Big Union, 1978

The PATRICIAS
A Century of Service

DAVID J. BERCUSON

GOOSE LANE EDITIONS

PRINCESS PATRICIA'S CANADIAN LIGHT INFANTRY

Edited by Barry Norris.
Cover and page design by Julie Scriver.
Printed in Canada.
10 9 8 7 6 5 4 3 2 1

Library and Archives Canada Cataloguing in Publication

Bercuson, David Jay, 1945-, author
The Patricias : a century of service / David J. Bercuson.

Includes an address by Adrienne Clarkson.
Includes index.
Co-published by: Princess Patricia's Canadian Light Infantry.
ISBN 978-0-86492-675-3 (bound). – ISBN 978-0-86492-462-9 (in slipcase)

1. Canada. Canadian Army. Princess Patricia's Canadian Light Infantry — History.
2. Canada. Canadian Armed Forces. Princess Patricia's Canadian Light Infantry — History.
3. Canada — History, Military.
I. Clarkson, Adrienne, 1939- , author
II. Canada. Canadian Armed Forces. Princess Patricia's Canadian Light Infantry, issuing body
III. Title.

UA602.P75B467 2013   356'.1130971   C2013-903050-6

Goose Lane Editions acknowledges the generous support of the Canada Council for the Arts, the Government of Canada through the Canada Book Fund (CBF), and the Government of New Brunswick through the Department of Tourism, Heritage, and Culture.

Goose Lane Editions
500 Beaverbrook Court, Suite 330
Fredericton, New Brunswick
CANADA E3B 5X4
www.gooselane.com

Princess Patricia's Canadian Light Infantry (PPCLI)
National Defence
PO Box 10500, Station Forces
Edmonton, Alberta
CANADA T5J 4J5

Contents

"To Our Fallen"

[top left] Princess Patricia of Connaught, CI, GCStJ, CD, 1886-1974; Colonel-in-Chief, Princess Patricia's Canadian Light Infantry, 1918-1974. [PPCLI RHQ]

[top right] Alexander Hamilton Gault, DSO, OBE, Russian Order of St Anne, Belgian Order of the Crown, three-times Mention in Dispatches; Founder; Honorary Lieutenant-Colonel, 1948; Colonel of the Regiment, 1958.

[bottom right] Patricia Knatchbull, Countess Mountbatten of Burma, CBE, MSC, CD, DStJ; Colonel-in-Chief, Princess Patricia's Canadian Light Infantry, 1974-2007.

[facing page] Madame Adrienne Louise Clarkson, PC, CC, CMM, COM, CD, FRSC (Hon), FRAIC (Hon), FRCPSC (Hon); Governor General of Canada, 1999-2005; Colonel-in-Chief, Princess Patricia's Canadian Light Infantry, 2007-present. [PPCLI RHQ]

From the Colonel-in-Chief

The pictures and text in this brief history tell the story of one of Canada's most illustrious regiments, Princess Patricia's Canadian Light Infantry.

This book depicts the remarkable story of how ordinary Canadians have performed with extraordinary commitment, skill, and gallantry in places as diverse as the mud and squalor of the trenches of France and Flanders, through Italy and northwest Europe, on bleak Korean hillsides, in Afghanistan's sweltering poppy fields, in traumatized countries around the world on peacekeeping missions, and on training grounds in Canada and Europe.

The Patricias are unique. They are a western-based regiment that has recruited men and women from every corner of Canada. They are an immensely practical and proud Canadian organization with a sensible flair for tradition. They have remained steadfast in an age that has often become jaded and cynical by pop celebrity and hype. As the pages of this book testify, the Patricias have embodied the qualities of loyalty, courage, commitment, duty, determination, and comradeship — and as one to have witnessed the Regiment close-up, as I have been privileged to do, I find these traits in the modern world very commendable. In their hundred years of history the Patricias have never lost the sense of who they are and what they stand for.

Uniforms, equipment, and tactics change profoundly; but as this book demonstrates, the spirit of the PPCLI endures. I am honoured to serve as the Patricias' Colonel-in-Chief. In the time I have been with the Regiment, I have become as confident of their future as I am proud of their past.

ADRIENNE CLARKSON
Colonel-in-Chief
Princess Patricia's Canadian Light Infantry

The Patricia Family

Princess Patricia's Canadian Light Infantry (PPCLI) has a unique and remarkable history as an infantry regiment of Canada's Army. It was founded by Andrew Hamilton Gault at the outbreak of the First World War and dedicated to the beautiful young Princess Patricia of Connaught, daughter of Canada's governor general. Gault's unique idea was to rally men from all over Canada with previous military service, most with the British Army, who might form an infantry battalion that could be dispatched to the war at the earliest opportunity. Over three thousand men answered Gault's call to arms and gathered in Ottawa where the Regiment was established. With a Camp Colour hand embroidered by the princess herself, these men were led into battle at the start of 1915 by Lieutenant-Colonel Francis D. Farquhar, a decorated British army veteran and first commanding officer of the PPCLI and by Gault himself as Farquhar's second-in-command. The regiment has served the nation with dedication, faithfulness, and courage in war and peace since then and in August 2014 will mark its first century of service.

From its very beginning, the PPCLI created a unique legacy that marked it off from all other regiments of the Canadian Army, and has emerged as a pillar both of the Canadian Armed Forces and of the nation. The Regiment's history is a story of tradition, valour, and sacrifice. It is also the story of a tightly knit military family, forged

primarily in the battles the Patricias have fought in all of Canada's wars since 1914 but combined also with the service of Regimental members wherever Canada has required them and whatever the challenge. This short book, in words and pictures, tells the story of the PPCLI, not only to mark the Regiment's first century but also to reintroduce Canadians to the Patricias' proud history. ∎

[top left] The Founder, Andrew Hamilton Gault, DSO.

[bottom left] H.R.H. Princess Patricia, circa 1916.

[top right] Princess Patricia and her parents, H.R.H. The Duke of Connaught, Governor General of Canada, and H.R.H. The Duchess of Connaught.

[facing page, l to r] Captain H.C. Buller, Adjutant, and Lieutenant-Colonel Francis Farquhar, DSO, Commanding Officer at Lansdowne Park, Ottawa, 1914.

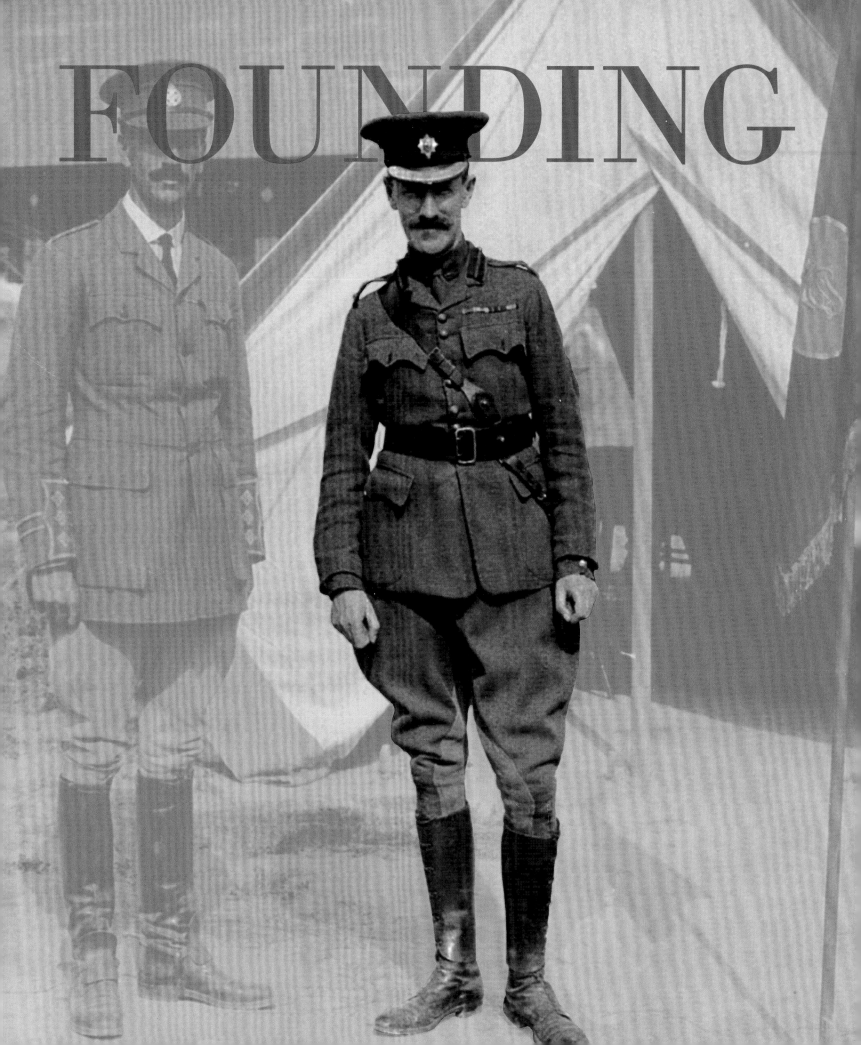

FOUNDING

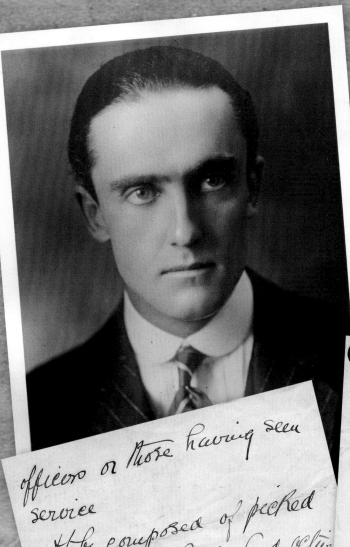

[left] The young Hamilton Gault met with The Honourable Sir Sam Hughes, Minister of Militia and Defence, in Ottawa on August 3, 1914, to discuss the possibilities of raising a regiment for service in the event that war broke out.

[below] Gault returned to Ottawa on August 5, 1914, to discuss the ideas for the creation of a regiment with Lieutenant-Colonel Francis Farquhar, Military Secretary to the Governor General of Canada. Note the possible insertion of 'Own' in the Regimental title.

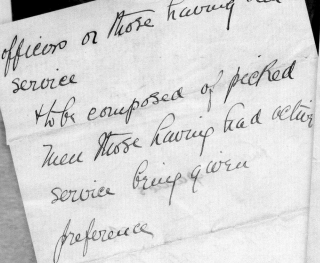

officers or those having seen service

+ to be composed of picked men those having had active service being given preference

waggon transport [require]

Own Canadian Princess Patricia's Light Infantry

4-27-1

CABLE ADDRESS "TRUNKCHAT"

Chateau Laurier

OTTAWA, CANADA.

A.T. Folger – Resident Manager

GRAND TRUNK · · GRAND TRUNK PACIFIC HOTELS

CHATEAU LAURIER, OTTAWA, ONT.   THE FORT GARRY WINNIPEG, MAN.
UNDER CONSTRUCTION
THE MACDONALD, EDMONTON, ALTA.   THE PRINCE RUPERT, PRINCE RUPERT, B.C.
THE QU'APPELLE, REGINA, SASK.

F. W. Bergman, Manager of Hotels Winnipeg, Man.

2 full companies
250 men each
+ correspond with British regular units

1 maxim unit

1 bearer company

to be commanded as far as possible by permanent force

Gault's Legacy

Andrew Hamilton Gault, the founder of the PPCLI, was born in Britain in 1882 but raised in Quebec. Six feet tall, well built, and ruggedly handsome, Gault loved the outdoors, and after he joined the 5th Royal Scots of Canada, a Highland infantry militia regiment in Montreal, he came to love military life. When war broke out in South Africa between the British Empire and the two Boer republics of the Transvaal and the Orange Free State in 1899, Gault enlisted with the 2nd Canadian Mounted Rifles. His unit left Canada for South Africa only in 1902, however, when the war was winding down, and Gault saw almost no action.

Gault's second chance to fight for the empire he so loved came with the outbreak of war in Europe at the beginning of August 1914. Canada, although fully self-governing in domestic matters, was still a British colony as far as foreign affairs were concerned, and Britain's declaration of war on Germany on August 4 meant that Canada was automatically at war as well. Gault had followed the breakdown of peace that began on June 28, 1914, with the assassination of the Austrian archduke Franz Ferdinand and his wife in Sarajevo and culminated with the German invasion of Belgium on August 3. On that very day, Gault travelled to Ottawa to offer Minister of Militia and Defence Sam Hughes to pay the cost of raising a cavalry regiment. Hughes convinced Gault that an infantry regiment would be more useful, but the subject was left unresolved when Gault returned to Montreal the next day.

[left] Lieutenant-Colonel Francis D. Farquhar, DSO, was the Military Secretary to the governor general of Canada in 1914. He was an officer of the Coldstream Guards and served in South Africa during the Boer War, 1899-1900, and was awarded a DSO, Mention in Dispatches, and the Queen's Medal with five clasps. He also served in Somaliland in 1903-04.

[facing page, top] H.R.H. Princess Patricia's note of acceptance and thanks for naming the Regiment after her.

[facing page, bottom left] H.R.H. Princess Patricia of Connaught, the youngest daughter of the Governor General of Canada, H.R.H. The Duke of Connaught.

[facing page, bottom right] The official letter of confirmation of the name of the Regiment, signed by Lieutenant-Colonel Charles Winter.

Lieutenant-Colonel Francis Farquhar, an experienced officer in the Coldstream Guards, was military secretary to the governor general, Prince Arthur, Duke of Connaught. Farquhar was eager to serve the empire, and Gault's proposal to Hughes gave him an opportunity. He wired Gault: "Come up at once, have got an idea." That idea, relayed to Gault on August 5, was to recruit an entirely new infantry regiment from among the many British and Canadian ex-soldiers then residing in Canada. This would serve two purposes. First, the new regiment would not draw men away from the Canadian Expeditionary Force (CEF), which Hughes was about to organize at Camp Valcartier, north of Quebec City. Second, the new unit would be ready for service quickly because the men serving in it would be veterans in no need of basic military training. Farquhar offered to command the new unit and thought Gault should be senior major

of the regiment and his second-in-command. He also suggested that the new regiment be named after the Duke of Connaught's daughter, Princess Patricia, a quiet, attractive, and popular woman of twenty-eight who was well known to Canadians because of her many travels around the country. She not only agreed with the proposition, but also provided the regiment, to be named Princess Patricia's Canadian Light Infantry, with a Camp Colour. Despite the official name, it was not a "light" unit with fewer men, less firepower, and more mobility than a "regular" infantry unit; rather, as Gault himself admitted, "light" simply added dash to the regimental name.

The agreement that Gault and Hughes worked out was based on Farquhar's idea. In return for a payment from Gault to the government of $100,000 — more than $2 million in today's money — Hughes pledged to help recruit the new unit largely by paying

be associated with it in this way, and to think that your corps will bear my name; and I wish to one and all in it the greatest success in their service for the

I need hardly say with what deep interest I shall always follow the progress of the regiment.

Believe me

Yours very sincerely-

Patricia.

9ᵗʰ Aug. 1914.

Dear Mr Gault.

My parents have readily acceded to your request that the regiment so generously being raised by you should be called after me. I am pleased and proud indeed to

Patricia
Colonel in Chief
P.P.C.L.I.
Feb. 1919.

Lady Patricia Ramsay CI CD

COLONEL - IN - CHIEF

PRINCESS PATRICIA'S CANADIAN LIGHT INFANTRY

MILITIA AND DEFENCE
CANADA

E

4-4-7

MINISTER'S OFFICE

OTTAWA. August 20, 1914.

Sir,-

I have the honour, by direction, to acknowledge Colonel Hughes' receipt of your letter of 13th instant, with reference to the name of the Princess Patricia's Regiment of Light Infantry.

Upon consulting the Chief of the General Staff and the Adjutant General I am informed that the style and title of the Battalion is "Princess Patricia's Canadian Light Infantry.

Trusting this will be satisfactory, I am,

Yours very truly,

Charles F. Winter

Lt.-Col.,
Military Secretary.

Hamilton Gault, Esq.,
Chateau Laurier,
Ottawa.

RECRUITS WANTED!

FOR
PRINCESS PATRICIA'S
CANADIAN LIGHT INFANTRY

RAISED BY A. HAMILTON GAULT, Esq.

COMMANDED BY LT:COL. F. FARQUHAR, D.S.O.,

(Coldstream Guards)

This unit will be equipped as soon as possible, and placed at the disposal of the Imperial Authorities.

Preference will be given to ex-regulars of the Canadian or Imperial Forces; or men who saw service in South Africa.

QUALIFICATIONS: (1) Physically fit. (2) Age limit, 40. (3) "Good" Certificates of discharge for ex-soldiers.

CONDITIONS: Enlistments for one year or the war. Pay Canadian Rate.

APPLY TO RECRUITING OFFICE WITHIN

[top left] On August 11, 1914, the machinery of recruiting went into action with the circulation of the recruitment poster. By August 19 the process of mobilization was complete and the Regimental strength of 1,098 was reached.

[bottom left] The Camp Colour was treated as a Regimental Colour from the time that Princess Patricia presented it to the Regiment. Here it is with a Colour party — carried by a subaltern with an armed escort of sergeants. Note the Ross rifles. The location could be either Lévis Camp, Quebec, or Bustard Camp in England prior to turning in the Ross rifles.

The Regiment, with the Pipe Band on parade, formed up for inspection on the infield of the track at Lansdowne Park, Ottawa. Note the inspecting party located at the rear platoon of the second group from the right (possibly No. 2 Company).

the cost of volunteers to come to Ottawa, where the Regiment would be formed. Hughes also agreed to equip the Regiment in the same manner and with the same weapons and kit as the CEF. The PPCLI would have the same establishment or structure as any other regiment in the Canadian or British Army. The government would also transport the Regiment to Britain, where it eventually would join a British brigade.

Men soon streamed into Ottawa from all parts of Canada, particularly the west, where many recent British immigrants had taken to farming or ranching. The Edmonton Pipe Band volunteered en masse to pipe the Regiment to war and back again. As the men arrived, they were put up on the grounds of Lansdowne Park. There was barely enough room for all. It was a chaotic time, with volunteers arriving, equipment coming in, and the need to house, clothe, and feed everyone. By August 19, less than three weeks after Gault had first proposed raising a regiment, Farquhar completed his selection. Almost one out of every three volunteers was chosen: 1,098 men, almost all of whom had had military service of some kind, with 456 actually having served in a war. The

[facing page, top] On August 23, 1914, Princess Patricia presented a Camp Colour to the Regiment on parade at Lansdowne Park. She was twenty-eight years old. In attendance were her parents, the Duke and Duchess of Connaught.

[facing page, centre] The Minister of Militia and Defence, Sir Sam Hughes, inspecting the Patricias at Lansdowne Park prior to departure on August 28, 1914.

The Regiment's officers in front of the Aberdeen Pavilion, Lansdowne Park, August 27, 1914. Notable in the picture are Lieutenant-Colonel Farquhar (centre), to the left is Major Hamilton Gault, and on the right Captain Buller. To the left of Gault is Lieutenant H. Niven, two further to the left is Major Pelly, and, on the far left, Captain Agar Adamson. Lieutenant Talbot Papineau is seated in the front row fifth from the right. All mentioned, except Papineau, who was KIA, would eventually command the Regiment.

No. 1288 Private Thomas Pritchard, an Original, proudly displaying the Camp Colour at Lévis Camp, Quebec, September 1914, prior to deployment overseas. He would survive the war and die in Toronto in July 1968.

explanation has its roots in the Highland tradition of the British Black Watch, which evidently called their Regimental Colour the *rikk u dan du*, a Gaelic term meaning "cloth of our mother." Speculation is that former members of the Black Watch serving with the Patricias gave the Camp Colour that name. Over time, it has evolved into Ric-A-Dam-Doo. Regardless, no one will ever be certain if this is the origin of the name. As the Princess passed the Colour to Farquhar, she declared: "I have great pleasure in presenting you with these colours, which I have worked myself. I hope they will be associated with what I believe will be a distinguished corps. I shall follow the fortunes of you all with the deepest interest, and I heartily wish every man good luck and a safe return." ■

majority — they were soon known as the "Originals" — were British born. At the Regiment's first formal parade at Lansdowne Park on Sunday, August 23, 1914, Princess Patricia presented the unit her handmade Colour: maroon with a circle of dark blue in the centre, on which her cipher, VP, surmounted by a coronet, was embroidered in gold thread. The Colour was soon affectionately called the Ric-A-Dam-Doo. The meaning of the name is shrouded in mystery but one

[facing page] Private Draycott, PPCLI, a veteran of the Boer War and a sniper when this photo was taken, later served on the 2nd Brigade Intelligence Staff. Wounded and gassed, he survived the war and received a Mention in Dispatches at the Somme in 1916. [CVA AM54-54:GRWarP.28]

[facing page, inset] The Regiment's first cap badge was designed around a marguerite flower. The choice was made by Hamilton Gault in recognition of his wife's name, Marguerite. The design drawings for the badge were prepared by Princess Patricia and are held in the Rideau Hall collection. [RHK]

[facing page, background] Courcelette, France, in ruins, as captured by the Canadian forces in 1916.

1914-1918

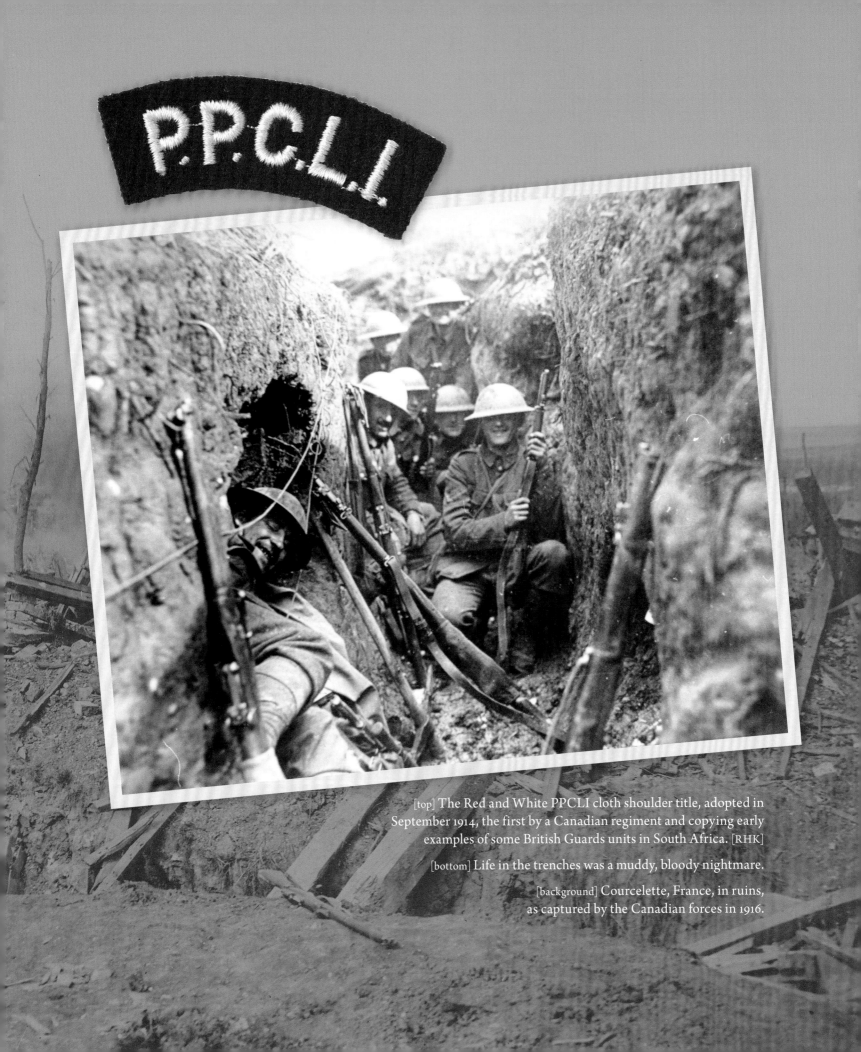

[top] The Red and White PPCLI cloth shoulder title, adopted in September 1914, the first by a Canadian regiment and copying early examples of some British Guards units in South Africa. [RHK]

[bottom] Life in the trenches was a muddy, bloody nightmare.

[background] Courcelette, France, in ruins, as captured by the Canadian forces in 1916.

The First World War

The Patricias left Canada on board the R.M.S. *Royal George* on September 27, 1914, and, after a brief stay in Britain, landed in Le Havre, France, on December 20. On the night of January 6/7, 1915, they entered a "quiet" sector along the southern perimeter of the Ypres Salient. As they moved closer to the trenches, the sights and sounds of war enveloped them. The countryside was torn up by shellfire, buildings were destroyed, the stink of rotting bodies and the sounds and flashes of explosions overwhelmed their senses. Then they took their first casualties. Sergeant Lewis Scott never forgot the moment the first two Patricias died: "We warned all ranks to keep their heads down....I heard a private named MacNeish say to his chum MacNeil, 'Mac, look at the bastards, they're bailing out too.'" Just at that time a rifle shot came, and when I got to where they were, MacNeish had been shot through the mouth and the front of MacNeil's face behind had been taken right off." The first officer killed was Captain D.O. Newton, who was shot in the stomach on January 7 and died the next day.

The Patricias were soon relieved, but returned to action on January 15 in the vicinity of St-Eloi. Their new trenches were worse than the ones they had first encountered: even when there was no rain the trench bottoms were covered in slimy mud, and when it rained the water rose quickly to thigh level. They were also narrow and crowded. Sergeant P.W. Candy later recalled, "where one man should have stood...we found that we were standing about eight men in the trench. It was a quagmire within two to three

The Regiment boarded the R.M.S. *Royal George* at Quebec City and departed in convoy on September 27, arriving in Plymouth on October 14.

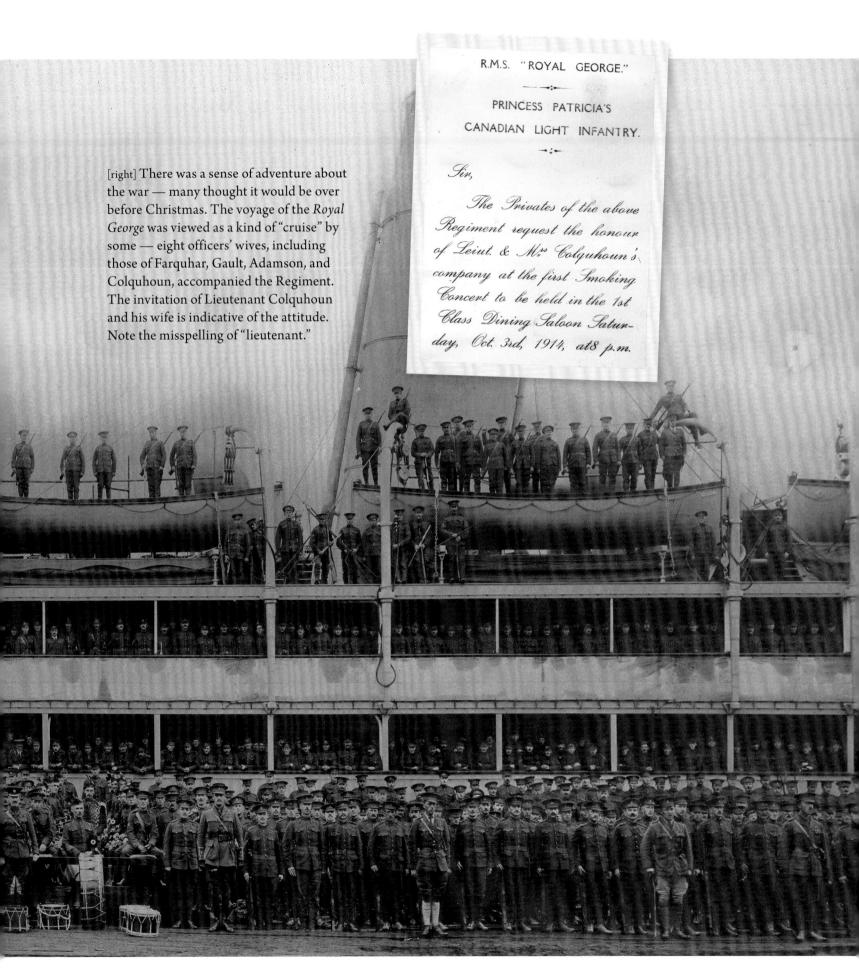

[right] There was a sense of adventure about the war — many thought it would be over before Christmas. The voyage of the *Royal George* was viewed as a kind of "cruise" by some — eight officers' wives, including those of Farquhar, Gault, Adamson, and Colquhoun, accompanied the Regiment. The invitation of Lieutenant Colquhoun and his wife is indicative of the attitude. Note the misspelling of "lieutenant."

R.M.S. "ROYAL GEORGE."

PRINCESS PATRICIA'S
CANADIAN LIGHT INFANTRY.

Sir,

The Privates of the above Regiment request the honour of Leiut. & M.rs Colquhoun's company at the first Smoking Concert to be held in the 1st Class Dining Saloon Saturday, Oct. 3rd, 1914, at 8 p.m.

hours." Constantly wet feet gave way to trench foot, a condition in which the flesh on the feet literally rots away, crippling the afflicted. Worse, so many men had been killed fighting over the same ground that almost every time the Patricias tried to dig new trenches or deepen existing ones, they unearthed rotting corpses. The pervasive stink of death merely added to the odour of stale water, mud, urine, and open latrines.

Ever-vigilant German snipers added to the danger of the sporadic shelling. Anyone careless enough to lift his head over the lip of a trench during daylight hours would be shot. Farquhar decided to equip some of the Regiment's best shots with rifles with sniper scopes and form special sniper units. The Patricia snipers studied their new craft diligently. Corporal Jim Christie from British Columbia learned how to camouflage himself and his rifle and how to use his scope to survey the enemy ground in front of him before carefully picking his target. The Patricia snipers got very good at their jobs, learning to spot enemy snipers, observe them, then kill them the instant an opportunity presented itself.

On the night of March 20, 1915, the Patricias were in their positions near St-Eloi, due to be relieved in place by a British battalion. Farquhar took the Commanding Officer of the relieving unit forward to give him an idea of what the front actually looked like before the units exchanged positions. Sergeant Louis Scott of the Patricias watched the two men move forward: "We were draining a front line trench...Colonel Farquhar was with the Colonel of the Rifle Brigade. They came up on an inspection tour to observe what was going on. He moved out just a little ahead of me, talking to the Rifle Brigade Colonel, when suddenly we heard him go down. He was shot with a stray bullet....We did what we could for him but obviously he needed to be into a dressing station and I ordered Sergeant Maclean and Sergeant MacMorris of my company with a stretcher to take him out to the dressing station at Vermacil, which they did. Regretfully, he died there."

Farquhar was buried the next evening at the PPCLI cemetery nearby. Major Herbert C. Buller, the Regiment's Adjutant, assumed command with the temporary rank of lieutenant-colonel (he was later officially promoted). Farquhar had helped Gault immeasurably to shape the Regiment and establish its earliest traditions. Now he was gone. Indeed, by the time the Patricias were ordered into reserve in the town of Ypres itself on April 17, at least three hundred of the men who had stood at the parade in Ottawa in August 1914 were dead, wounded, or casualties of what was then known as "shell shock." Yet the PPCLI still had not seen a general action.

Then, on April 22, the Germans launched a heavy attack on the northern flank of the Ypres Salient using chlorine gas for the first time in the war. For more than a week, Germans, French, British, and Canadians clashed in what became known as the Second Battle of Ypres. By May 2, when their last attack petered

The Death of Colonel Farquhar

The day after Colonel Francis Farquhar was buried, Lieutenant (later Major) Talbot Papineau wrote to his widow: "There is not a man in the Regiment who does not feel a great and personal loss. No other man in so short a time could have won so much respect and affection. As a Canadian I feel a national debt of gratitude to him. An Imperial officer who could have commanded the highest position in the English army, he accepted the task of creating, as well as commanding, a new and untried Canadian Regiment…He is no longer with us, but his influence and his memory will endure with the life of the Regiment."

[top] The shell of the Cloth Hall still standing amid the destruction of Ypres, 1917.

[bottom right] Original burial marker at Voormezeele of Lieutenant-Colonel Farquhar, killed in action at Shelley Farm, near St-Eloi, France, March 20, 1915. The PPCLI grave marker in the background marks the burial place of Lance Corporal N. Fry.

[top] The men at the top left throwing grenades are Privates J. McCormack and J. Kelly; the machine gunner is Corporal C. Dover, with Private L. Phillips to his right and further to the right is Private G. Candy. Lieutenant Hugh Niven is yelling with his hand to his mouth as Corporal A.G. Pearson, at left, carries an ammunition box. The wounded man sitting at the bottom of the trench is Sergeant John McDermott. William Barnes Wollen (British, 1857-1936), *The Canadians Ypres*, 1915, oil on canvas, 111.8 x 165 cm. [PPCLI NAA2701]

[bottom] A group of Originals after the Battle of Frezenberg, 1915.

[top right] The Patricia position during the Second Battle of Ypres, April-May 1915, was on the Bellewaerde Ridge, immediately east of Bellewaerde Lake. It's remembered in the Regiment as the Battle of Frezenberg, named for a town at the crossroads north of the Patricia position. [PPCLI RHQ]

[bottom left] A typical scene of the devastation, near Bellewaerde Ridge, caused by prolonged artillery bombardment.

out, the Germans had not captured the town but they did succeed in pushing the line back about three kilometres, rendering the British positions on the rim of the Ypres Salient untenable and in danger of being outflanked. British commander Sir John French thus decided to shrink the entire salient, and the Patricias withdrew from their positions on the southern part after dark on May 3.

In their new positions just to the east of Belle-waerde Ridge, itself part of Frezenberg Ridge, the Patricias were repeatedly and heavily shelled. On May 5, Buller was hit in the eye by a shell fragment, and Gault took command temporarily; Lieutenant Hugh Niven, who had joined the PPCLI at the very start from the Middlesex Light Infantry, a militia regiment, was appointed adjutant, and Agar Adamson took over as second in command. Throughout May 7, Gault did what he could to strengthen the position and deploy the Patricias in the event of a major German attack. The attack he anticipated came early the next morning, as the normally sporadic enemy shelling suddenly increased to a torrent that ranged over the whole position before concentrating on the two companies in the forward trenches.

W.J. Popey was in the No. 2 Company position when the heavy shelling began. "We were rudely awakened the morning of the 8th by a shell bursting

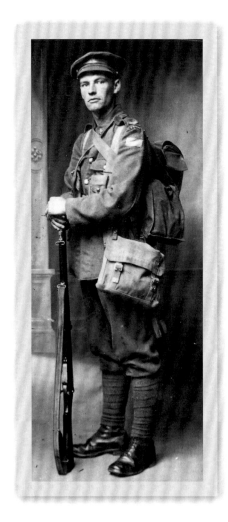

Private N. Clarke in field marching order.

The Patricia survivors in the front trenches did what they could to drive the Germans back, but there were too few of them left alive or able to hold a rifle. The Germans continued to advance, bayoneting every wounded Patricia they found, as J.J. Burke later recalled. On the left flank of the Patricia position, the British 83rd Brigade of the 28th British Division began to collapse. The Germans swept into the hole left in the British line and turned the PPCLI's left flank. With Bellewaerde Lake at their backs, the Patricias fought with Gault in command. Soon after, however, Gault was seriously wounded in his left arm by shrapnel. About a half-hour later, he was hit again, this time in the left thigh and much more seriously. Hustled to a position in the support trench, Gault passed in and out of consciousness as the battle raged around him. He refused any suggestion that he be evacuated ahead of any other of the wounded. It would take months for him to recover and rejoin the Patricias.

With Gault out of action, Captain Agar Adamson took command, but he too was soon hit in the left shoulder. Still, he carried on, reorganizing the Patricias' defences on the left flank with rifle and machine-gun fire covering the gap left by the now-departed 83rd Brigade. At the same time, he struggled to help bring ammunition to his beleaguered men: "Even today, I can see Captain Adamson with one arm hanging down getting ammunition from the dead and dying and handing it to us," Bill Popey

in our lean-to artillery dugout," he later remembered. "One man, I forget his name, sat with his head off. He had been cleaning his rifle. Most of us had been hit by fragments of shrapnel. We all rushed out and got into the trench. A piece [of shrapnel] had cut through my belt and was rubbing my side. Wright dug it out and I helped some of the others. From that time on it was hell, so many things happened. The shells landed thick and fast. We were down hugging the ground." Jimmy Vaughan, another soldier in the forward position, was stung by the ferocity of the attack: "Everything was blown to pieces. There were no trenches left... [we] were fighting on nerve."

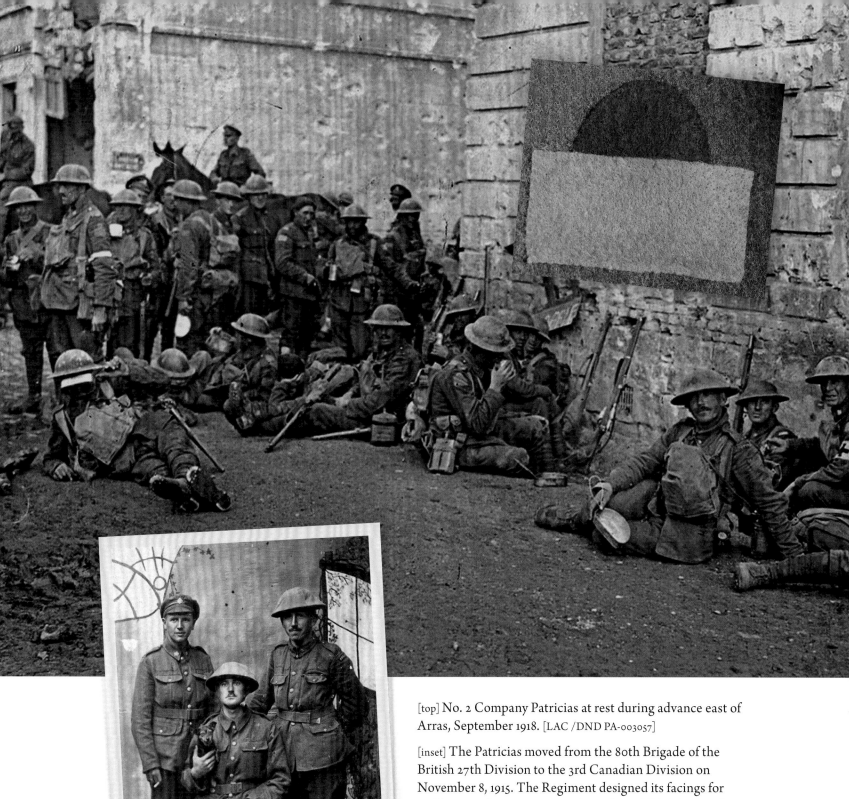

[top] No. 2 Company Patricias at rest during advance east of Arras, September 1918. [LAC /DND PA-003057]

[inset] The Patricias moved from the 80th Brigade of the British 27th Division to the 3rd Canadian Division on November 8, 1915. The Regiment designed its facings for uniforms and accoutrements from the 3rd Division patch of French grey. [RHK]

[bottom] Three Patricias relax out of the line, perhaps at Steenvoorde, June 1916. Two of the three are F.C. Dohanney and, with the tiny dog, H.C. Rickaby, who was awarded the French Croix de Guerre after the Battle of Amiens in 1918.

would remember many years later. Under Adamson's leadership, the Patricias held.

At about 10:30, the PPCLI counterattacked and momentarily succeeded in driving the Germans back, but heavy casualties made the situation of both forward companies unsustainable, and Adamson ordered them to the rear. The support trench linking the forward and rearward positions was choked with dead and wounded men, so the survivors of the two forward companies had to make their way back over open ground. At noon a company of British soldiers worked their way forward to the PPCLI, bringing two machine guns and thousands of rounds of small-arms ammunition. Adamson deployed the machine guns and most of the British soldiers on the PPCLI's left flank, then tried, but failed, to link up with British troops still holding the line on the other side of the gap.

In the early afternoon, other groups of British reinforcements made their way into the PPCLI positions, to be deployed by Adamson as the battle raged on. The Germans launched their last major attack of the day in mid-afternoon. Again the Patricias held, but many of their trenches had been blasted to bits, and dead and wounded lay scattered across the position. Wounded men who could still fire their rifles stood beside the few who were unscathed and shot the Germans down as they came. Then, toward late afternoon, the German attack faltered. Adamson handed command to Lieutenant Niven, who held on until the Patricias were relieved at dark.

As Niven led the Patricias out, the Ric-A-Dam-Doo came with them. The Camp Colour had been shot through, possibly when Regimental Sergeant Major A. Fraser (one of the first men to enlist) was killed as he stood on the parados of the trench serving out ammunition and directing fire. Most of the Original Patricias did not survive the battle. Niven led four officers and one hundred fifty men out of the support trench and back along the Ypres-Menin road on the night of May 8/9; the official history of the PPCLI lists 392 killed, wounded, or missing in the day's fighting. The Patricias' action on May 8 is immortalized in regimental history as the Battle of Frezenberg. The Regiment marks May 8 with an annual parade or trooping of the Regimental Colour.

The battle changed the composition of the Regiment. With some 70 per cent casualties and the Regiment reduced to the size of a single company, replacements were badly needed. Back in Canada the need was met by the "University Companies Reinforcing PPCLI," originally organized by two McGill University graduates whose intention was to recruit at McGill and other universities to form a reinforcement draft for the Patricias. Eventually more than twelve hundred students were sent to the PPCLI in six company-sized drafts. The new PPCLI was thus a unique mix of weary veterans, mostly of working class origin, who had survived the worst the Germans had thrown at them, and fresh-faced, educated young Canadians who were mostly from well-to-do

The 1st University Company was formed in spring 1915 from students at McGill University on the initiative of two graduates, George C. McDonald and Percival Molson. The Company joined the Regiment on September 1, 1915, near Armentières, France. Identified in the picture are privates Dougall, Fraser, MacPherson, Lynnons, and Hardy (Hardie).

families. Although the two groups were from disparate backgrounds, their strengths complemented each other nicely and formed a special bond of trust. By the end of the war, three-quarters of these student recruits would be killed or wounded.

The university recruits were a temporary answer to the Regiment's larger question of where to find replacements. The British Army felt no obligation to Gault to provide British recruits even though the Regiment was part of the British Expeditionary Force (BEF) — indeed, it was having trouble enough filling its own rapidly expanding ranks. Quite simply, no one had anticipated that men would be killed or wounded so quickly and in such large numbers. In addition, the British 27th Division was about to be ordered to the Middle East to join the campaign in the Dardanelles against Turkey. Gault, Buller, and others, therefore, decided to accept an invitation to switch the Regiment from the BEF to the Canadian Expeditionary Force, which was in the process of forming the 3rd Canadian Division. On November 25, 1915, the PPCLI was officially placed under the command of the Canadian Corps and assigned to the 7th Canadian Brigade, which also contained the Royal Canadian Regiment and the 42nd and 49th Battalions, from Montreal and Edmonton, respectively.

Through the remainder of 1915, the Patricias saw only "light action," although light action on the Western Front was a constant rotation in and out of the front trenches and daily casualties from shell and rifle fire and clashes in no man's land. The Regiment saw heavy action once again, however, in early June 1916 in the Battle of Sanctuary Wood. Colonel Buller was killed in the fighting, and command once again devolved on Gault, who was himself badly wounded in the left leg. Again, as at Frezenberg, he refused evacuation while the fighting raged, insisting on directing his regiment from a stretcher. But this time his wound was much more serious than any of his

The Patricias at Courcelette

"It was pitiful to hear the wounded moaning," one Patricia later recalled. W.M. Oliver was luckier than many of these men: "I went over with the first wave, but after I had gone about fifty yards or so I got hit in the arm, but I thought it didn't matter, and that, if I went back to the dressing station, I should be thought trying to get away from the danger zone. Or in other words, scared. So I crawled as best I could through a communication trench and went on ahead, which proved to be the better choice, as numbers were killed who were on their way to the dressing station."

Soldiers line up at the Trench Shop run by the YMCA, 1917.

earlier afflictions, and his leg was later amputated in a London hospital.

The Patricias, along with the rest of the Canadian Corps, were fortunate to avoid the slaughter of the early months of the Battle of the Somme and did not see heavy fighting until September 15, as the Battle of Sanctuary Wood continued. This clash was only a small part of a much larger struggle known to history as the Battle of Mount Sorrel, which itself was one of the closing actions in the Battle of the Somme. At the town of Courcelette, the Regiment suffered 307 casualties in roughly twenty-four hours on September 15 and 16. Three days later, the Canadian Corps was withdrawn from the Somme fighting, and left the Ypres Salient. By early spring 1917, it was in position at the foot of Vimy Ridge, with Agar Adamson now in command of the Patricias. The Canadian mission was to take the ridge and, in so doing, to succeed where both the French and the British had failed before.

The Canadians were well prepared. Large tunnels were dug in the chalk at the foot of Vimy Ridge to give cover to the troops, who would need to advance from their trenches to their start line for the attack. The Patricias were assigned to Grange Tunnel, which they entered on the night of April 8. There they waited until the pre-dawn of

[right] Jenny MacGregor Morris opened her home to Patricias who found themselves in London either on leave or recuperating from wounds.

[far right] Patricias and other Canadian soldiers at 34 Bedford Street, London, the home of the Regiment's "London Mother," Jenny MacGregor Morris.

Easter Monday. Their immediate goal was to advance straight up the hill and capture two German trenches, one seven hundred metres away and the other four hundred metres farther on. Sometime during the night it began to snow as the wind picked up. As the first streaks of dawn appeared, machine guns opened up on the German positions. Then, a massive bombardment, a creeping barrage, thundered through the air and shook the ground. On Adamson's orders, the PPCLI pipers led the assault companies up the ridge as No. 1 and No. 3 companies and fifteen thousand other Canadians in the first wave began their advance.

The pipers marched about eighteen metres in the snow, and then returned to the tunnel to help carry the wounded. The rest of the Patricias continued the arduous climb over broken ground in the driving sleet. Most of the Germans in their path had been killed, wounded, or rendered senseless by the bombardment,

but many defenders remained to harm the advancing Canadians.

All along the 3rd Division front, the attacking infantry followed the creeping barrage into and over smashed and battered German positions. German soldiers surrendered by the dozens. The two lead Patricia assault companies were quickly followed by No. 2 and No. 4 companies, who charged up the slope bare minutes after the initial assault wave left the trenches. All four companies reached their initial objective within an incredible thirty minutes, then went on to take the second in less than half an hour, suffering fewer than fifty casualties, taking one hundred fifty prisoners, and clearing the crest of the ridge. In their new position they discovered the entrance to a German bunker, fitted with mirrors, wash basins, and chairs. There were bunks, some

Vimy Ridge

Andre Bieler was in the assault wave at Vimy Ridge: "We were loaded with wire, we were loaded with tools…it was difficult to advance especially because of the craters which we had to go down into and up again." George Hancox recalled: "We started to go forward following the lip of the crater and past the German outposts which by then were non-existent. Heavily laden we lumbered along through the maze of shell holes over the obliterated German front line, past more and bigger shell holes until we reached the main German defensive line, which was the first objective."

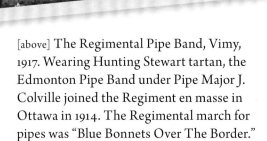

[above] The Regimental Pipe Band, Vimy, 1917. Wearing Hunting Stewart tartan, the Edmonton Pipe Band under Pipe Major J. Colville joined the Regiment en masse in Ottawa in 1914. The Regimental march for pipes was "Blue Bonnets Over The Border."

The Regiment moves into line at Vimy-Mericourt Road led by the Pipe Band and the Ric-A-Dam-Doo, June 27, 1917.

covered with fine blankets, and dozens of bottles of wine and mineral water. It was a stark contrast to the way the Canadians had lived for much of the war.

The Patricias, along with most of the attacking companies of the 1st, 2nd, and 3rd Divisions, had completed their assigned task in record time with relatively few casualties, but the battle was not over yet. As Adamson wrote to his wife the next day, "We took all our objectives yesterday pushing off at 5:30 A.M. in a rainstorm. The 4th Division on our left, not yet in line with us…failed in two attempts to gain their objective. We have our flank in the air and are suffering from enfilade fire in newly dug trenches…I think we can hang on. Our Brigade did splendidly." In the end, the Patricias lost eighty-three killed on Vimy Ridge and brought out one hundred thirty-nine other casualties. The Canadian Corps as a whole suffered 3,598 killed and 7,004 wounded in the two-and-a-half-day battle, but unlike previous costly attacks that had often seemed senseless, Vimy Ridge was a brilliant success for the Canadian Corps and a triumph for the PPCLI.

Less than three months later, the Patricias descended into the hell of Passchendaele. British Field Marshal Douglas Haig's objective for this major effort of 1917 was to attack from the Ypres Salient to the northeast, capture Passchendaele Ridge, then mop up the German positions all the way to the Channel coast. Like the Battle of the Somme of the previous summer, however, the campaign quickly bogged down into a months-long battle of attrition in the rainiest weather seen in years, which, combined with incessant shelling, turned the battleground into a deep and muddy morass. To make matters worse, the Germans had prepared a formidable belt of defences in front of Passchendaele village, anchored on concrete pillboxes with interlocking fields of fire.

The Canadian Corps entered the Battle of Passchendaele on October 26 with an attack on Passchendaele village; the Patricias did not take part. The second phase of the Canadian attack began on October 30, this time including the Patricias, who were led by No. 2 Company on the right, under the command of Captain M. Ten Broeke, and No. 3 Company on the left, commanded by Major Talbot Papineau. The other two companies followed close behind. It had not rained for two days, but the mud had not dried to any significant degree, making it impossible for the Regimental pipers to play the men over the top as they had done at Vimy. The Patricias climbed from their forward trench at zero hour and struggled to follow the slowly moving barrage. They were met immediately by a storm of machine-gun fire. Then the Germans opened their defensive barrage on the slowly advancing Canadian infantry. Papineau looked over the battlefield as he climbed from his trench and said to Niven, the Regiment's second in command, "You know, Hughie, this is suicide." Moments later a shell cut Papineau in half. As the men struggled toward their first objective, a pillbox dubbed Duck Lodge,

Passschendaele

Two days after the Patricias pulled out of the battle, Adamson wrote his wife: "The ground we gained and held against two counter-attacks and continuing artillery bombardment is of some importance, as the ridge we took is a commanding one.... The higher authorities are themselves out in expressing to us their appreciation of our efforts, but I can't help wondering if the position gained was worth the awful sacrifice of life."

[top] A typical scene of the Passchendaele battlefield over which the Patricias advanced.

[bottom right] Talbot M. Papineau, MC, great-grandson of Louis-Joseph Papineau, leader of the 1837 Rebellion and cousin of the Quebec nationalist Henri Bourassa, was a PPCLI Original. He received a Military Cross at St-Eloi in 1915 and was one of four lieutenants left in action at the end of the Battle of Frezenberg. He was killed at Passchendaele on October 17, 1917.

they were mowed down like wheat. Virtually all the officers were hit within the first hour. The Patricias pushed ahead, but the 49th Battalion on their left flank was unable to keep up. The plan called for the two units to coordinate an assault against the heavily defended Meetcheele crossroads, but the handful of Patricias who reached that point reached it alone.

One pillbox in particular was the key to the defences. Lieutenant Hugh McKenzie, a Patricia attached to the 7th Machine Gun Company, hurriedly put a plan together: he and a small party of men would divert the German machine gunners' attention while others would try to take the position from the flank and rear. One of those others was Sergeant G.H. Mullin, who charged the pillbox, bombed out a handful of snipers in front of it, and leapt onto its roof. With bullets ripping through his overcoat, he shot two machine gunners with his revolver and then assaulted the entrance. The Germans surrendered. The night before this feat, while Mullin was distributing the evening's rum ration, he had told one of his men, "I'm fed up to the teeth. Tomorrow morning it's either a wooden cross or a VC for me." For capturing the pillbox single-handed, he was awarded one of the first two PPCLI Victoria Crosses; the second went posthumously to McKenzie, who did not survive his almost suicidal effort to draw the Germans' fire.

The Patricias took the crossroads, but they were unable to push on to their final objective, Graf Farm, only some three hundred metres to their right — there were simply too few men left standing. Adamson called off the assault and ordered the men to dig in for the inevitable German counterattack. Of the six hundred or so who started out on the morning of October 30, one hundred fifty-nine had been killed and two hundred four wounded, most within the first few hours. Adamson was stunned by the losses. Regimental Runner Andre Bieler remembered seeing him at battalion HQ "in such a state of tension...the loss of a regiment was just too much."

In late February 1918, the regiment received the news that King George V had appointed Princess Patricia Colonel-in-Chief of the PPCLI. The move had come after Canada had pledged that the PPCLI would be retained after the war as a unit in Canada's Permanent Force. The pledge was due recognition not only of Gault's efforts to create the Patricias, but also of the unit's strong bond to the Empire and its now overwhelmingly Canadian character, a symbolic transition under fire. The PPCLI thus became the second of three Canadian permanent regiments in the Canadian Infantry Corps that survive to this day.

In March 1918, Agar Adamson, age fifty-two, relinquished command of the Patricias to Major Charles Stewart, whom Gault thought of as a man "who would fight the battalion boldly and well in any kind of action." Then, in May, the Patricias, along with the rest of the Canadian Corps, began to prepare for

[top] A ward in the PPCLI Canadian Red Cross Hospital at Bexhill, England, 1918.

[top right] The Victoria Cross, the highest military decoration awarded in the British Commonwealth for valour in the face of the enemy. [RHK]

[top far right] Lieutenant Hugh McKenzie, VC, DCM, planning an operation with his warrant officer. McKenzie, who served as a non-commissioned officer before becoming a lieutenant in early 1917, was awarded the Victoria Cross posthumously for his action at Meetcheele Ridge on October 30, 1917, during the Battle of Passchendaele.

[centre right] Sergeant George Harry Mullin, VC, MM, awarded the Victoria Cross for his action at Meetcheele Ridge on October 30, 1917, during the Battle of Passchendaele. He survived the war and died on April 5, 1963. Born in Portland, Oregon, he is one of only five Americans who have been awarded the VC, all in the First World War. A sixth was awarded to the Unknown Soldier buried in Arlington National Cemetery, near Washington, D.C.

[bottom right] Sergeant Robert Spall, VC, awarded the Victoria Cross posthumously for his action on the night of August 12-13, 1918, during the Battle of Parvillers. [Canadian War Museum 19910109-743]

The Regiment, under the command of Major Stewart, provides an Honour Guard for H.R.H The Duke of Connaught on June 27, 1917, at Camblain l'Abbé, France. Also visible is the Canadian Corps commander, Lieutenant-General Arthur Currie. [LAC/DND PA-001903]

a massive offensive involving artillery, tanks, and aircraft, aimed at breaking through the German lines and pushing on toward the German border.

The initial attack was aimed at Amiens, a city opposite the Canadian lines. The attack began on August 8, but the Patricias did not go into action until ordered to advance on the village of Parvillers late on August 11. By then, the Germans there had overcome the shock of the August 8 attack and resisted fiercely. At one point No. 3 Company found itself cut off as German attackers closed in on two sides forcing the company to retreat down the trench. One platoon, however, found itself in grave danger of being overrun. Platoon Sergeant Robert Spall grabbed a Lewis gun and leaped onto the parapet, pouring magazine after magazine of .303 bullets into the German troops, who went down by the dozens. Spall then jumped back into the trench and led his platoon to the safety of a sap some seventy-five metres away. He then grabbed

a second Lewis gun, scrambled onto the parapet again, and again loosed a stream of bullets into the Germans. He held them long enough for the platoon to get away, but was then shot dead. His posthumous Victoria Cross was the third and final VC won by a Patricia in the Great War.

Canadian Corps commander Lieutenant-General Sir Arthur Currie called off the attack on August 15 and shifted the Corps' focus to another axis of advance. The offensive resumed eleven days later. On September 28, the Patricias were passing through the hamlet of Raillencourt, on the north side of the Arras-Cambrai road, when they were heavily shelled. Lietenant-Colonel Stewart was killed, the third Patricia commanding officer to be lost in action. He was replaced, first, by Captain J.N. Edgar, then by Captain G.W. Little.

As the grind toward the Belgian city of Mons continued, the Patricias were losing hundreds of men

PLAYER'S CIGARETTES.

PRINCESS PATRICIA'S · CANADIAN LIGHT INFANTRY ·

CANADA.

[top left] Card placed in packages of Player's cigarettes to honour the Regiment. On the back it notes that the PPCLI was the "first Canadian regiment to join the British Expeditionary Force in France. It has suffered more casualties and seen more fighting than any other Canadian Unit."

[top right] Sergeants from No. 4 Company, PPCLI, out of the line at St-Hilaire, France, undergoing a long course of specialized training, June 1918.

killed and wounded. On September 30, for example, they and the 49th Battalion attacked the heavily defended town of Tilloy, which they cleared but at the cost of sixty-six dead and two hundred ninety-three wounded. The Canadian Corps' drive continued, but the Patricias were too depleted to carry on for the moment. Acting Major A.G. Pearson was promoted to the rank of acting Lieutenant-Colonel and given

command of the Regiment on October 16. Pearson had joined the PPCLI as a private.

The PPCLI returned to the front lines in early November. By then, Germany was on the verge of collapse, but the Germans in Mons, still the object of the Canadian Corps' drive, fought on. On November 10, most of the PPCLI was withdrawn from the fighting and replaced in the line by the Royal Canadian Regiment, but No. 4 Company was left in the midst of the battle, attached to the 42nd Battalion.

Commanding 13 Platoon of No. 4 Company when it crossed the canal and entered Mons was W.J. "Bill" Popey, who had left Calgary in early August 1914 to join the Patricias in Ottawa — one of the few remaining Originals. On the night of November 10/11, he and his platoon were locked in heavy street fighting in the centre of the city when orders came from 42nd Battalion HQ to pull his men back and get them into billets for the night: "John Christie and I went to the

Hamilton Gault's Dedication to His Regiment

Hamilton Gault was wounded in action three times, losing his leg the third time. He was then forced to relinquish command of the Regiment, although he regained it briefly after the fighting and brought it back to Canada in 1919. He formally, and for the last time, relinquished command on January 20, 1920. But even as a staff officer at 3rd Canadian Division during the Last Hundred Days, he could not resist appearing on the battlefield on horseback to cheer his regiment on. After the war, he made light of his amputation by naming his wooden leg Herbert and a spare leg Hubert. Gault returned to the land of his birth in the early 1920s and enjoyed a successful career in British politics, then served as a staff officer with the Canadian Army in Britain during the Second World War. Gault stayed in close touch with the Patricias after the war and maintained a deep interest in Regimental affairs, helping to safeguard Regimental heritage and aid the governance of the Regimental Association. In 1948 he was appointed Honorary Colonel of the Regiment and, in 1958, the year of his death, Colonel of the Regiment. He was succeeded by Cameron Ware, who had commanded the PPCLI in action for a significant part of the Italian campaign and who served until 1977.

[right] Hamilton Gault with Princess Patricia, 1919.

[facing page, far right] Honorary Major the Reverend T. McCarthy, MC, officiated at the consecration of the Ric-A-Dam-Doo from Camp Colour to Regimental Colour on January 28, 1919, at St-Léger, Belgium.

Lieutenant-Colonel Gault leads the Regiment
in three cheers for the Colonel-in-Chief,
H.R.H Princess Patricia, at its final inspection,
Bramshott, England, February 21, 1919.

[top left] Lieutenant-Colonel "Hammie" Gault, DSO, with General Plummer on horseback in the Mons city square, November 11, 1918.

[top right] One hundred fifty Patricias take part in a composite parade for the formal entry of General Sir Henry Horne, Commanding General British First Army, Mons, November 15, 1918.

big hotel past the depot, an old man let us in through the downstairs door," Popey later remembered. "We got into an old fashioned white sheeted bed in our clothes with our boots on. We awakened at 11:15. John [was] looking out the window [and] said 'My God Bill, the Germans must be back.' We went downstairs. The old proprietor met us, kissed and hugged us both and gave us a bottle of champagne each. This was the first we had heard of the Armistice." Popey had beaten the odds only to sleep through the end of the war.

The PPCLI suffered 4,076 killed, wounded, and missing in the course of the war, in effect replacing itself four times over. Three commanding officers were killed in action. Three Patricias were awarded

the Victoria Cross for gallantry, while three hundred sixty-six other decorations were distributed to members of the Regiment. When the 3rd Division paraded in the centre of Mons on the afternoon of November 11 to salute the Canadian commander, Arthur Currie, thoughts of home and survival were no doubt uppermost in the minds of the men who passed before him. First in the field of Canadian units, the PPCLI had been in the thick of virtually every major battle the BEF and the CEF had fought on the Western Front, creating a tradition of valour, dedication, and sacrifice that has marked the Patricias ever since. ■

[facing page] Lieutenant Rex Carey, A Company, receives the Military Cross from General Sir Bernard Montgomery, later Field Marshal, commander of the British Eighth Army, at Cantanzoro, Italy, 1943, for actions performed at Leonforte on July 22.

[facing page, inset] Polished bronze Marguerite. [RHK]

[facing page, background] Regimental tent lines in a bivouac at Dunfermline, Scotland, 1940.

1919-1945

[top] The Regiment arrived in Ottawa on March 19, 1919, to be greeted by the Governor General, The Duke of Devonshire. The men then moved to Lansdowne Park for demobilization.

[centre right] Hamilton Gault and Lieutenant-Colonel M. Ten Broeke, MC, Commanding Officer, at an A Company parade, Fort Osborne Barracks, Winnipeg, 1927.

[bottom right] The oldest private in B Company, Private D.W. Cuthbert, the company storeman, age 62, with thirty-two years, seven months of service, and the youngest, Boy E.P. Shaw, age 16, with six months of service. Although he went on to be a warrant officer second class, Shaw was known throughout his service as "Boy Shaw."

[background] The Regiment returned to Canada aboard the R.M.S. *Carmania,* arriving in Halifax on March 17, 1919. The Patricias arrived at the CPR station in downtown Ottawa on March 19.

P. P. C. L. I.

OLDEST and YOUNGEST

Pte. D. W. CUTHBERT
Age — 62 years.
Service to date —
32 years, 7 months.

Boy E. P. SHAW
Age — 16 years.
Service to date —
6 months.

The Inter-war Years and the Second World War

On November 22, 1918, Hamilton Gault returned briefly to lead the Patricias back to Canada. The government's plan for the post-war army was to retain the Royal Canadian Regiment in Ontario and the Maritimes, transform the French-speaking 22nd Battalion of the CEF into the Royal 22nd Regiment in Quebec — affectionately nicknamed the Van Doos — and station the Patricias initially in Winnipeg at the Fort Osborne Barracks and later also at Work Point Barracks in Esquimalt, British Columbia. The Permanent Force regiments, vastly reduced in size from their wartime establishments, were to aid the civil power when necessary and train the militia across entire regions of the country. The west was the responsibility of the PPCLI. B Company of the Patricias, stationed in Esquimalt, was assigned to train units in British Columbia and Alberta, A and D companies in Winnipeg were to train the militia in Manitoba and Saskatchewan (D Company was disbanded in 1924). C Company was not "stood up," or activated, until Canada mobilized for war in 1939.

As a Permanent Force regiment, the Patricias began to enshrine the PPCLI's traditions — some born of its founding and others arising from its battle honours — in the accoutrements and practices that made up Regimental lore. For example, in late January 1919, Princess Patricia's Camp Colour was consecrated at a religious ceremony in Belgium. The Regiment also met Princess Patricia herself at Bramshott Camp in southern England on February 21. The princess, who had returned to Britain for her

[top left] A one-hundred-man PPCLI Guard of Honour, with the Ric-A-Dam-Doo, under command of Major M. Ten Broeke, MC, at Princess Patricia's wedding to Commander A. Ramsay, DSO, RN, at Westminster Abbey on February 27, 1919. Afterwards she relinquished her Royal title and was known as Lady Patricia. [LAC/DND PA-006267]

[bottom left] The Wreath of Laurel. [RHK]

[top right] H.R.H. Princess Patricia attaching the Wreath of Laurel onto the Ric-A-Dam-Doo, Bramshott, England, February 21, 1919. Note the worried look on the corporal's face.

[bottom right] In the best traditions of the Regiment, an NCO takes the initiative and steps forward to assist the Colonel-in-Chief.

marriage to Commander A. Ramsay of the Royal Navy (thereafter being known as Lady Patricia Ramsay), inspected the Regiment, read out a message of farewell, then placed a laurel wreath in silver gilt on the staff of her Colour. All officers and a representative group of non-commissioned offers (NCOs) attended her wedding six days later before the Regiment boarded ship for Canada. The Patricias arrived in Ottawa on March 19 and paraded through a cheering crowd to Connaught Square for an official greeting by the governor general before marching to Lansdowne Park for their official dismissal. With characteristic

unselfishness, dignity, and dedication to his beloved regiment, and despite his wooden leg, Gault led the Patricias on the three-kilometre march before bidding them goodbye. Arriving at Lansdowne Park, Gault read a final Order of the Day to the Great War Patricias. Barely able to control his emotions, he proclaimed: "I believe we have all returned to Canada better fitted to take up the duties and responsibilities of citizenship in the Country we love so well. Difficult days may lie before us...but if they are faced with the same steadfastness of purpose which has characterized the years we have passed through, I feel confident that you will succeed in whatever you may undertake to do."

With the PPCLI officially reactivated as a regiment of the Canadian Army on April 1, 1919, and with the

[top] B Company, on parade at Work Point Barracks, Esquimalt, British Columbia, 1922, Major Francis H.M. Codville, MC [foreground], in command and [behind him] Captain J.S. Woods, MC. CSM Edward Ryan is on the right flank of the formation, and Major Dameril A. Clarke is on the left flank. To the far left are the canteen and guard room, in the centre is the engineer building, and on the extreme right is the Royal School of Instruction building.

[bottom right] Kit laid out for daily morning inspection, 1928, Fort Osborne Barracks, Winnipeg.

B Company PPCLI, inspection in field marching order, Work Point Barracks, Esquimalt, 1930. Company Sergeant Major Sidney Mitchell stands to the right in the centre. The building immediately to the left is the Warrant Officers' quarters; farther down the line are the sergeants' quarters. The B Company office is immediately behind the tent.

[top left, l to r] Smokey Green, George Wilkinson, Hugh Kelly, and Ossie Newbury at Sarcee Camp, near Calgary, circa 1936. Lance Corporal Wilkinson and Private D. Cessford (not in the image) were the first Patricias in action in the Second World War when they crewed anti-aircraft guns on a British trawler in the Irish Sea in June and July 1940. Note the style of rolling the puttees with the top half in "vees." Only the other ranks did this; officers rolled them straight. [GW]

[facing page, top left] A crew under the command of Corporal Frank Loveless practise mortar drill: (l to r) unknown, Dick Whittington, unknown, Vic Rawlings. Not a real mortar, this practice model was fabricated in the local Army Ordnance workshop, Esquimalt. [GW]

[facing page, top right] Privates Mart Larson sending and Dick Whittington recording signals transmitted by heliograph, Work Point Barracks, Esquimalt, circa 1936 or 1937. Larson was the first Patricia killed in the Second World War.

[facing page, bottom right] B and C companies form up in field marching order for final inspection at Work Point Barracks, Esquimalt, November 12, 1939. Two days later they departed for Winnipeg.

[top right] The Regiment receives new Colours from the Governor General, The Earl of Bessborough, PC, GCMG, at Minto Armoury, Winnipeg, April 14, 1934, replacing the original Ric-A-Dam-Doo. The field officer for the King's Colour was Major Colquhoun and for the new Regimental Colour Major D.A. Clarke, MC. The subaltern for the new Regimental Colour was Second Lieutenant H.F. Cotton and for the Kings Colour, Lieutenant P.B. Coristine (not visible).

battlefield demands of the Great War behind them, the Regiment's leaders now faced the unique challenges of peacetime. The Regiment's establishment was now a fraction its wartime size, and lack of money meant that collective training opportunities were severely limited. The Patricias thus had to rely on enthusiasm and imagination to maintain acceptable levels of professionalism. Despite these crippling restrictions, the Patricias trained the militia, embarked on an intensive and enterprising sporting schedule to keep fit, went on exercise whenever money permitted, and kept up a rigorous social and regimental life. Most often, Patricias travelled by train in ones and twos to outlying communities throughout British Columbia

56   The Patricias

[right] Officer Cap Badge, 1935-1956. [RHK]

[far right] Lady Patricia Ramsay and Hamilton Gault hold the new Regimental Colour, in the new College of Heralds design, with the First World War Battle Honours emblazoned on its field of French grey.

[facing page, top] B Company on parade in celebration of the Coronation of King George VI, Major J.N. Edgar, MC, commanding.

[facing page, centre left] A section of A Company lines up for inspection by the General Officer Commanding Military District #10, Fort Osborne Barracks, Winnipeg, October 28, 1937.

[facing page, centre right] The Escort for the Colour passing in front of the saluting base during the Trooping of the Colour, Fort Osborne Barracks, Winnipeg, 1937.

[facing page, bottom] The Regiment parades with the Regimental brass band through the streets of Winnipeg, 1938, led by Lieutenant-Colonel W.G. "Shorty" Colquhoun, MC. The brass band was established as part of the Canadian Permanent Force in 1919.

and across the prairies in an effort to keep the militia at an adequate level of proficiency in drill, tactics, and elementary weapons training. The training visits by PPCLI officers and NCOs were highly valued by their militia counterparts. Throughout the 1920s and 1930s, Patricias ran "Royal Schools" at Heals Rifle Range in Saanich, British Columbia, and across western Canada, where future militia leaders, most of whom served without pay, were trained as instructors and studied tactics on cloth models and "tactical exercises without troops." It was a kind of soldiering with unique difficulties, one that demanded patience, far-sightedness, and good humour, qualities the Patricias had in abundance. Their years of perseverance were to serve Canada well.

When war broke out again in September 1939, Canada was woefully unprepared. The Regiment, though quietly professional and fully understanding the enormity of the task before it, was, in a material sense, far from ready for battle. The Nazis, in contrast, had been assiduously equipping and preparing their nation for war.

It was a warm Indian summer's day in Winnipeg when the Patricia's CO, the near-seven-foot tall legendary leader of Great War fame, Lieutenant-Colonel "Shorty" Colquhoun, received a curt telegram reading "Reference Defence Scheme Number Three, Mobilize Entire Force." With the odds stacked against it and a bleak and uncertain future ahead, the Regiment

[top] PPCLI Rifle Team, Fort Osborne Barracks, Winnipeg, 1936.

[background] A motorcycle escort in full dress, under the command of Captain R.L. Mitchell, was provided for the cross-Canada tour of King George VI and Queen Elizabeth, 1939.

[top] A section of PPCLI undergoing training at Sarcee Camp, near Calgary. The Regiment continued to wear the colonial-style Wolseley pith helmets well into the 1930s, primarily for ceremonial occasions. The Regiment also conducted field training at Shilo, Manitoba, and at Heals Rifle Range, Saanich, British Columbia.

[top left] Hamilton Gault met the Regiment on its arrival at Morval Barracks, Cove, near Farnborough, on December 30, 1939. Gault was promoted to brigadier in 1942 but ill health forced him to retire that year.

[top right] The Colonel-in-Chief, Lady Patricia Ramsay, officiating at a change of command parade between Lieutenant-Colonel W.G. Colquhoun, MC, and Lieutenant-Colonel J.N. Edgar, MC, September 14, 1940. Edgar is to the left of Lady Patricia and Hamilton Gault is to her right front. Colquhoun was later promoted to brigadier and appointed commander of the 7th Canadian Brigade.

once again undertook the challenge with the professional and resolute spirit that had characterized it since its birth. Colquhoun and his officers plunged immediately into the massive job of turning what was essentially a peacetime, barracks-style, regiment back into a wartime fighting force. On September 10, Canada declared war on Germany for the second time in a quarter-century. Princess Patricia's Canadian Light Infantry was to face the travails and the dangers of another all-out war.

The implementation of Defence Scheme No. 3 meant two things for the Patricias: the Regiment would be brought up to its wartime establishment of about 835 men as quickly as possible and concentrated at Fort Osborne Barracks in Winnipeg, and it would be assigned to the 2nd Canadian Infantry Brigade of the 1st Canadian Infantry Division, which was to be sent to Britain as quickly as possible. Each of the division's three infantry brigades would consist of a Permanent Force battalion as the core along with two Militia battalions. The Patricias would serve alongside the Seaforth Highlanders of Canada from Vancouver and the Edmonton Regiment from Edmonton for the rest of the war.

"Shorty" Colquhoun oversaw the task of recruitment, and by the end of August the PPCLI two company establishment of three hundred men had been increased to a wartime strength of four companies totalling eight hundred. The two west coast companies joined the Regiment at Fort Osborne Barracks on November 15, and the entire Regiment,

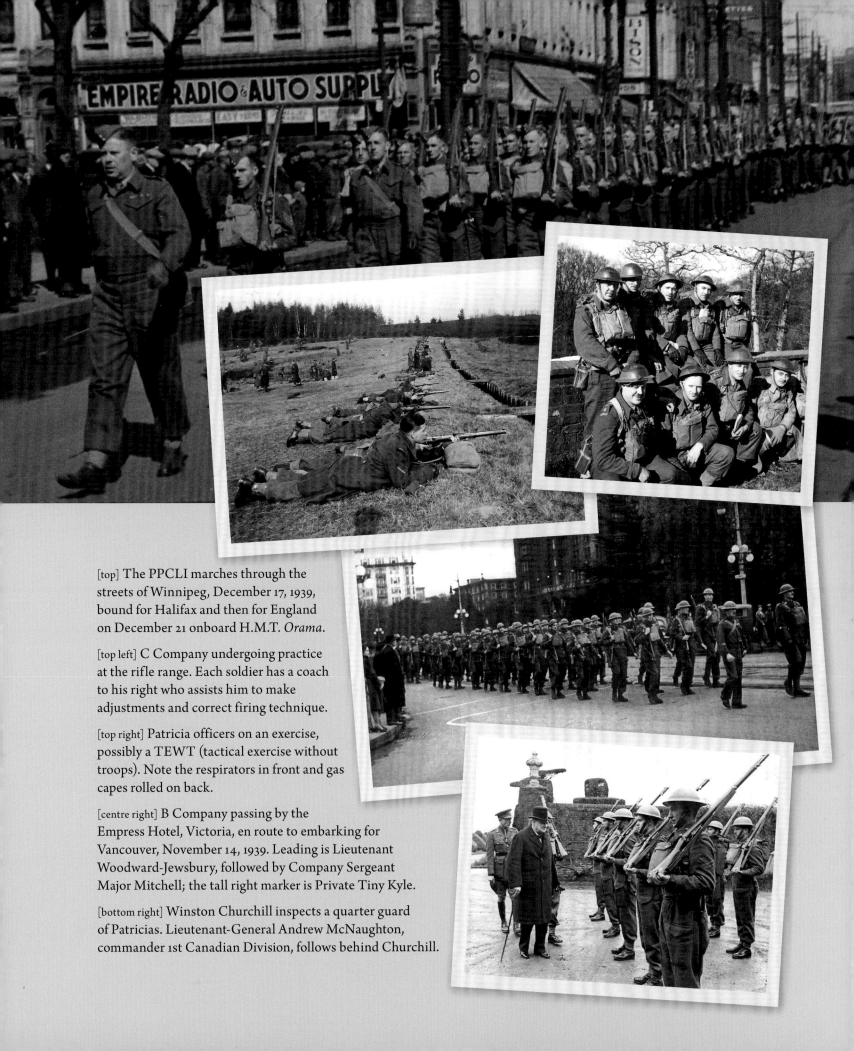

[top] The PPCLI marches through the streets of Winnipeg, December 17, 1939, bound for Halifax and then for England on December 21 onboard H.M.T. *Orama*.

[top left] C Company undergoing practice at the rifle range. Each soldier has a coach to his right who assists him to make adjustments and correct firing technique.

[top right] Patricia officers on an exercise, possibly a TEWT (tactical exercise without troops). Note the respirators in front and gas capes rolled on back.

[centre right] B Company passing by the Empress Hotel, Victoria, en route to embarking for Vancouver, November 14, 1939. Leading is Lieutenant Woodward-Jewsbury, followed by Company Sergeant Major Mitchell; the tall right marker is Private Tiny Kyle.

[bottom right] Winston Churchill inspects a quarter guard of Patricias. Lieutenant-General Andrew McNaughton, commander 1st Canadian Division, follows behind Churchill.

now four rifle companies strong, departed by train for Halifax on December 17. Boarding H.M.T. *Orama*, the Patricias arrived at Gourock, on the west coast of Scotland, on December 30. From there, they were taken by train to southern England, to the same area near Aldershot where the Originals had first encamped in the Great War. They were greeted by Hamilton Gault, who had been appointed commander of the Canadian Reinforcement Depot in Britain, and by Brigadier George Pearkes, a VC-winning veteran of the First World War who had been appointed to command the 1st Canadian Infantry Division.

These Patricias were very different from their forebears. For one thing, they were mainly Canadian born. For another, the majority had no military experience whatever. At the core of the Regiment were the three hundred men who had served in the Permanent Force in the inter-war years, some of them veterans of the Great War. The rest were either militiamen or recruits who had joined literally off the street. Thus, the homogeneity that had marked the Originals was missing. And although some of the Patricias had been inculcated with Regimental traditions in the inter-war period, most had little or no knowledge of how the Regiment was founded or the role it had played in the Great War.

On September 9, 1940, "Shorty" Colquhoun left the PPCLI to assume command of the 7th Brigade and was replaced with a succession of commanding officers, including the Great War veteran J.N. Edgar, until R.A. Lindsay, a militia officer from the South Alberta Regiment, who had transferred to the Patricias in November 1939, assumed command. For the next three and a half years Lindsay trained the Patricias for battle while Ottawa wrestled with the question of where and when the Canadian Army should be committed to the fight. Finally, in March 1943, Ottawa notified London that Canada was now ready to send a division into the fray wherever it might be needed. The British asked to use a Canadian infantry division and a Canadian armoured brigade in "operations based on Tunisia." Ottawa readily agreed.

In early May 1943, Lindsay received a warning order that the Regiment would soon be on the move to Scotland for "combined operations" (amphibious) training. For the balance of May and the first four weeks of June, the Patricias trained hard in the art of assault landing, one of the most dangerous and difficult operations in warfare. On May 21, the practice landings ended and the Regiment entrained for Hamilton, near Glasgow, where it began to load assault gear into transports. Trucks, radio equipment, rations, ammunition, jeeps, medical supplies — all had to be loaded in such a way that, when the Regiment hit the beaches, the first items needed would come out of the transports first. The Patricias' woollen battledress was taken away and replaced with khaki shirts and shorts. "It was obvious that we were going to a fairly warm climate," Sydney McKay later recalled. "Of course that just made us all try to guess where." Finally the men were issued malaria tablets, one a day for eight days as a starting dose.

The Patricia Landings at Pachino

Captain Donald Brain, in command of B Company, later wrote about the Patricias' Italian landing: "As we approached the shore flares could be seen.... Machine gun tracer made attractive patterns against the sky. On shore every once in a while there would appear a bright flash followed by a loud report...the shore gradually became clearly defined and the order was given for the landing craft to deploy. On touchdown the doors were dropped and the men disembarked in water well above their waists. In a few instances they had to swim for it." Chester Hendricks was one of those Patricias who started their war with a good soaking: "Chester...was carrying a Bren gun and stepped off the end of the gangway and down he went," Andy Schaen later recalled. "He disappeared. He came up, but the Bren gun didn't."

Patricias disembark from a landing ship at Pachino, Sicily, July 10, 1943. [LAC/DND PA-114889]

On June 14, the Patricias boarded the troop transport *Llangibby Castle* to continue last-minute amphibious training. They stowed their gear and lived aboard ship in Greenock harbour for two weeks while a large convoy gathered around them. On June 28, Brigadier Chris Vokes, who had been in command of the 2nd Brigade since May 1942, came aboard along with Major-General Guy Simonds, commander of the 1st Canadian Infantry Division, for a visit and inspection. Ever the dramatist, Vokes charged his officers to "fight to the death" in the forthcoming operation. Then, at 9:30 p.m., with the sun still hanging in the northwestern sky, the convoy weighed anchor and steamed out to sea. Operation HUSKY — the assault on Sicily — was about to begin, and the Patricias would be in the first wave.

In the pre-dawn hours of July 10, 1943, the PPCLI, along with the rest of the 1st Canadian Infantry Division, landed at Pachino, on the southern tip of Sicily. There were no Germans anywhere near the Canadian beaches, and the Italians showed almost no fight at all. In the first two days, the PPCLI suffered just five wounded. The Regiment's greatest challenges were the extreme heat, the dust, the mosquitoes, and the lack of transport. Many of the division's wheeled vehicles and artillery were at the bottom of the sea, sunk by a German submarine. So the Patricias had to advance inland on foot, climbing in the hot sun, bitten by bugs, their arms and knees sunburned, much of their equipment carried by mules hired from local muleskinners. They had been aboard ship for four

Mayor Frost of Ispica

Ispica, a town of thirteen thousand inhabitants near the Canadian landing beaches, surrendered after a short naval bombardment. Lieutenant Sydney Frost of the Patricias was assigned to occupy the town with his platoon. The first residents he met were a nervous mayor and police chief, accompanied by several townspeople offering wine and fruit. Frost grabbed his Italian phrasebook and uttered a greeting. The Italians had no idea what he was saying and suggested they switch to French, which Frost had learned in high school. The encounter was an auspicious start to Frost's career as mayor: "At the ripe old age of twenty-one, I had taken over the administration of a town of more than 13,000 inhabitants without any real authority from my superior officer or anyone else. During the next two weeks I ran the town with hardly any outside help, not even from the headquarters of my own…Battalion, still 15 miles away in Pachino near the beaches. But I thoroughly enjoyed every minute and concluded that perhaps a benevolent dictatorship was not, after all, a bad thing!"

weeks with very limited exercise, and they now felt every kilometre of their push along winding roads into the high hills of central Sicily. The division marched north through one small town after another — Ispica, Modica, Ragusa — before finally running into the German rearguard at Grammichele on July 15; the

1st Brigade cleared the town several hours before the PPCLI passed through it. Caltagirone and Piazza Armerina were next, on July 17. In the first week of the invasion, the PPCLI had suffered only two killed and ten wounded, fewer than were felled by illness.

The overall Allied plan for the Sicilian campaign was to have the British under General Bernard Montgomery push up the east coast to capture Messina and trap the Italian and German soldiers on the island. The Canadians would guard the British left flank and the Americans, landing on the beaches to the left of the Canadians, would take much of western Sicily. But the British ran into very heavy German opposition near Mount Etna, while the Americans under General George Patton swung west to take Palermo, then began an eastward drive along the north coast to beat the British into Messina. Since Montgomery's forces were stalled, he ordered Simonds to push the 1st Canadian Division up the middle of the island, outflank the Germans, then turn eastward to link up with the British on the coast. Simonds's big push began on the night of July 17, with the 1st Brigade leading the way once again. The 2nd Brigade followed after initial German opposition was overcome, and the PPCLI advanced through Valguarnera, then mounted a short and successful flanking attack on July 19 to help the Seaforths.

Early on the 20th, the 2nd Brigade began its effort to take Leonforte. The approach to the town was along a twisting road that descended to a steep ravine, where

[top] A PPCLI section ambushes a German transport convoy during the advance to Enna, Sicily, July 22, 1943.

[left] Patricias advancing, Valguarnera, Italy, July 1943. [LAC/DND PA-130216]

the road bridge had been destroyed by the Germans, then climbed into the southern part of the town. The Seaforths were first to try it, but were forced back by intense German fire. The Loyal Edmonton Regiment followed (they had received the designation "Loyal" the previous month) and made it into the town, but were cut off. Then it was the PPCLI's turn. The engineers had succeeded in building a new bridge over the ravine, so C Company of the Patricias would be accompanied by four tanks, quadruple-mounted anti-aircraft guns, and anti-tank guns.

In the pre-dawn darkness of July 23, the Patricias waited as the column prepared to push off to relieve the Loyal Eddies and take the town. As first light began to erode the darkness in the eastern sky, they heard shells rumbling overhead and saw explosions blossom across the ravine and on the approach to the objective. The column began to move, down the

road, and across the bridge. German fire increased as it pushed into the centre of town. Lieutenant-Colonel Lindsay, the commanding officer, sent A and B companies to reinforce the assault. A Company, under Major J.R.G. Sutherland, pushed through Leonforte to the heights above. The fighting was intense and personal with grenades, rifles, and bayonets until the Germans were pushed out of their defensive positions. Leonforte was the Patricias' first real battle of the war. They lost thirteen killed and nine wounded.

The Canadians now began to push eastward, toward Adrano, the key to the German defences around Mount Etna. They were fighting crack troops determined to make the Canadians pay for every metre of advance. The hilltop villages and towns, twisting roads, and innumerable ravines gave the German defenders the advantage of terrain. But they were executing a fighting withdrawal with no reserves

[top] A section of C Company, led by platoon commander Lieutenant Gordon Sellars, approaching Adrano, Sicily, August 22, 1943.

[left] Lieutenant A.M. Campbell and Sergeant W.D. Carmichael discuss plans during a rest period near Militello, Sicily, August 21, 1943.
[LAC/DND PA-130214]

to hold a defensive line across the island. It was only a matter of time before the Allies secured Sicily, but much hard fighting remained. On July 26, the PPCLI reduced two German positions astride the highway west of Agira, allowing the rest of the 2nd Brigade to pass through. Then it was on to Agira itself, where the PPCLI followed a creeping barrage into the town. The Germans put up only sporadic resistance. On August 3, the 1st Brigade took Regalbuto, while the 2nd Brigade was assigned to secure three peaks to the north of the highway. Vokes, the 2nd Brigade's commander, ordered Lindsay to take one of these peaks, Monte Seggio. The Patricia attack did not get rolling until after daylight on August 5, but by then the Germans had all but pulled out of their defensive positions. After this action, Lindsay was replaced by

Cameron B. Ware, a Permanent Force officer who had graduated from Royal Military College (RMC) in Kingston, Ontario, before joining the Patricias in 1935.

Monte Seggio was the last action in Sicily for the PPCLI. In the northeast sector of the island, the curtain was falling on the battle as the Americans and the British pushed through to Messina and the Germans withdrew. The PPCLI encamped at Militello, near Catania, on August 11 and remained there while preparing to cross the Strait of Messina to begin the drive up the Italian mainland.

The Patricias, along with the rest of the 2nd Brigade, crossed the strait on September 4 and, after occupying Reggio di Calabria, the capital of Calabria, on the coast, followed the leading 3rd Brigade up the centre of Italy's "toe." In the meantime, the 1st Brigade

Cameron Ware

Cameron Bethel Ware was born in London, Ontario, in 1913. He joined the PPCLI in 1935 after graduating with a commission from the Royal Military College of Canada in Kingston, Ontario. After a brief exchange with the British Army, he was promoted to major with the Patricias in 1940 and to second-in-command in 1941. He became commanding officer of the Patricias in July 1943 and remained in command until he was replaced after the Battle of the Hitler Line. As CO, Ware focused on training and strengthening Regimental loyalty as preconditions for effective performance in action. He quickly earned the trust and loyalty of the Patricias and developed a legacy for Regimental command second only to that of Hamilton Gault himself. In fact, Ware communicated with Gault numerous times during the war, keeping him informed of Regimental events and sharing his appreciation of the Patricias' progress in combat. Ware was awarded a Mention in Dispatches in October 1943 and was presented with the Distinguished Service Order following the Battle of the Moro River in December of that year. Ware also had a distinguished post-war career in the Canadian Army and was officially appointed Colonel of the Regiment in September 1959, a post he held until April 1977. He retired from active service with the Canadian Armed Forces in September 1966 and died on January 21, 1999.

Lieutenant-Colonel Ware receives the Distinguished Service Order from Lieutenant-General Sir Oliver Leese, KCB, CBE, DSO, commander of the British Eighth Army, for actions performed on December 5, 1943, in the Moro River campaign near Villa Rogatti, Italy. Note the censors' mark on Ware's shoulder title.

moved straight into the mountains and pushed over the high Aspromonte range toward Loci, on the far side of the "toe." The weak Italian opposition caused few delays; blown bridges and blocked roads accounted for most of the wasted time. As Sydney McKay remembered, "We never ever got too far without finding blown bridges and these bridges were over ravines, more than over water but they still had to be bridged before we could move on."

As the Canadians drove north toward Potenza, they found the countryside here almost idyllic and mostly untouched by war. Canadian Army war artist Charles Comfort later noted: "The grape harvest was going on everywhere. The principal native traffic of the road was concerned with the harvest and with wine. The grapes were contained in large tubs, carried on low wagons. As we passed, bunches were thrown at us, sweet and lush." The people were poor

and desperate after having had their crops seized by the Germans. They were also suffering the ravages of war for the first time. But they were remarkably friendly, and for the most part, the Canadians formed strong bonds with them. One night in the mountains of Reggio Calabria, the Patricias heard singing and celebrating from a nearby village. In the morning they learned that the Italian government under Marshal Badoglio had surrendered. That was good news, of course, but the Patricias soon learned that the surren-

der hardly counted; the Germans had always been the real opposition in Italy and, as yet, they were nowhere to be found.

On October 14, the 1st Canadian Infantry Division entered the mountain town of Campobasso unopposed and billeted there until November 29, when they began to pull out and head for the Adriatic coast. The Canadians were to occupy positions vacated by a British division that had suffered many casualties as it pushed across the lower Sangro River in heavy fighting. The Canadian task: assault across the Moro River and capture the small coastal town of Ortona, about three kilometres farther on. By December 4, the Patricias found themselves in their new positions on a ridge overlooking the south bank of the Moro. They had had an easy war so far, with just thirty-four killed in action or dead on active service and one hundred thirty-nine wounded since landing in Sicily nearly five months earlier — the Originals had suffered more casualties in a single hour at the Battle of Frezenberg.

Midnight, December 5/6, 1943: the Patricias' objective in the first wave of the assault across the Moro was the small town of Villa Rogatti. The Regiment was supposed to follow a creeping barrage down into the valley of the Moro, across the river, and up a narrow path to the town, but the artillery was cancelled at the last moment. Ware boldly decided to push on anyway. Downstream they could hear firing as the Seaforths began their part of the attack. Incredibly, despite all the firing up and down the river, the Germans in Villa Rogatti were caught by surprise. The Patricias were almost into the town when the Germans woke up and started firing, but after four hours of shooting and grenading, the PPCLI broke into the centre of town. A troop of British Sherman tanks moved into Villa Rogatti after first light while the PPCLI prepared for the expected German counterattack. The Germans launched two that day, one in the morning and the other in early afternoon

accompanied by armour. The British tankers and the Patricias beat off both attacks. Ware later recalled the second: "It was a fair massacre. We allowed them to come … within fifty metres before anti-tank fire was opened." When it was all over, the PPCLI war diarist noted: "After nearly sixty hours of fighting and 'standing to' the troops are beginning to look tired. The strain and excitement has keyed them to a pitch higher than … any previous battle during the Italian campaign."

The 1st Brigade took over the task of securing the north bank of the Moro before the 2nd Brigade was called upon to cross a deep gully that lay across the path of its attack. The head of the "Gully," as it would thereafter be known, opened on the Adriatic about a kilometre south of Ortona, where the ravine ran deep and narrow. Winding back about six kilometres, the gully gradually rose to meet the surrounding ground. Overgrown with bushes, brush, and old vineyards and strewn with garbage, it offered an excellent defence. Not only was it a natural tank trap, it was also a perfect reverse slope, and gave the Germans ample cover for weapons pits and firing trenches laid out so as to catch advancing infantry silhouetted against the sky if they even got near the Gully's edge. The guns of the Canadian artillery could not be elevated high enough to destroy the German positions dug in on the south bank of the Gully. But before the Canadians could even get to the Gully, they would have to cross a rise known as Vino Ridge, running along the south edge

"I have not been out of my clothes for three
weeks.... Guess you know all about that
feeling! The fighting has been pretty bitter and
a different proposition from the early days of
Italy and Sicily. The Hun is stubborn and has
lots of guts and skill. Have lost many fine men
and officers but it's been a grand show...we
have not changed from the time of 1914 and
we are never stopped and we never give any
ground...they are so proud of being Patricias
and I am so proud of them and I hate losing
any of them."

[top] Officer Collar Badge, 1920-present. [RHK]

[bottom] 1st Canadian Infantry Division formation
patch. [RHK]

of the Gully, and they would have to do it over open ground and in the face of intense German fire. The Patricias were assigned the task.

For four days, the PPCLI attacked Vino Ridge against the fierce resistance of well-dug-in elements of a German parachute regiment. Jack Haley would later describe the ridge in words reminiscent of Passchendaele: "As time went on you looked out at the battlefield and the scene on those cold, wet, sort of drizzly days, and it was bleak. The shell holes were everywhere...There were broken houses, rubble and splintered trees and worst of all there was the mud. We were bogged down many times and the ground was all churned up and it really slowed us down." The Patricias were exhausted, their ranks depleted and they were low on ammunition and rations. Brigade commander Chris Vokes finally switched the axis of

attack, sending the Van Doos inland to capture the village of Casa Berardi and outflank the Gully. The Germans pulled out, and the PPCLI occupied the ridge and stayed there while the Loyal Eddies and the Seaforths fought the terrible battle of Ortona.

The Patricias and the rest of the 1st Canadian Infantry Division wintered on the Adriatic coast near Ortona, but in the spring headed inland to join the Allied offensive to capture Rome by pushing up the Liri Valley. Ware led them into action again on May 23. Accompanied by the tanks of the North Irish Horse, the PPCLI was assigned to attack on the right (north) flank of the 1st Canadian Division right through the formidable German defences of the Hitler Line along the southwestern bank of the Aquino River. The ground was a German kill zone with thick belts of barbed wire strewn with anti-personnel and anti-tank

[top] Patricias disembarking from Buffalos after crossing the Ijssel River, Netherlands, April 11, 1945. [LAC/DND PA-133333]

[left] Stretcher bearers evacuating casualties from A Company headquarters, north of Ortona, Italy, January 20, 1944. [LAC/DND PA-130862]

mines and with machine guns well forward to protect the wire; well-sited anti-tank guns supported concrete pillboxes that formed the main line of German resistance. The attack began just before six a.m. but bogged down almost immediately. The tanks blew up one by one and the Patricias began to fall by the dozens. Ware radioed brigade headquarters that his unit was in desperate shape, but he was told to hang on because the attack was going very well on other fronts. In twelve hours the PPCLI suffered fifty-nine killed, one hundred eighteen wounded, and seventeen taken prisoner — the Regiment's costliest battle in the entire war. The attack, however, was the beginning of the end of the German fight for Rome, which fell to the Allies on June 5.

The next day was D-Day, the invasion of Normandy. Henceforth, northwest Europe was to be the focus of the Allied thrust in the west, and Italy gradually became a sideshow designed to pin down as many Germans as possible and prevent their being shifted to other fronts. Virtually all the Allied replacements of men and equipment now would go first to northwest Europe, and the men fighting in Italy deprecatingly nicknamed themselves the "D-Day Dodgers."

The fight for Italy thus dragged on for the Patricias and the other soldiers of 1 Canadian Corps. With hard fighting in the month of June, the PPCLI suffered a further sixty-two men killed in action or dead of wounds, six missing, and two hundred thirty-five wounded. Then, from October 20 to 23, the Patricias and the rest of 1 Canadian Corps forced a crossing of the Savio River as they drove toward Bologna. Nine more Patricias were killed, forty-nine wounded, and fourteen taken prisoner. The fighting continued as they crossed the Ronco River, the Naviglio Canal, and finally the River Senio, where the Canadians held up for the winter. There, the PPCLI patrolled and endured the cold and wet until February 25, 1945, when it was relieved by a British battalion. The Patricias left Italy behind them and were sent to Holland for what would be the last major Canadian battle of the war: an attack by the entire First Canadian Army, reunited for the first time since summer 1943, to complete the liberation of the Netherlands.

The last major Patricia action of the war took place in April 1945. On the 11th, the PPCLI and the Seaforths led the 1st Canadian Infantry Division in an attack across the Ijssel River, some five kilometres south of the town of Deventer. Riding British Buffalos — tracked amphibious vehicles — across the river, they took the Germans by surprise. Two days later, they led a further push to a point about fifty-five kilometres west of the Ijssel, where the entire Canadian Army stopped at a predetermined separation-of-forces line to allow food aid to be trucked into what was left of starving, Nazi-occupied Holland. On April 30, Hitler shot himself in his bunker in Berlin as Soviet troops closed in on his headquarters in bitter fighting to take the German capital. By the time Hitler's successor, Grand Admiral Karl Doenitz, agreed to unconditional surrender, the Third Reich was in a state of collapse. The last shots on the PPCLI's

front were fired on May 5; all other German forces laid down their arms on May 7.

Thus did the Second World War pass into Regimental history. Hamilton Gault wired Patricia CO, Lieutenant-Colonel R.P. Clarke, just after the fighting ended: "You have magnificently maintained the traditions of your Regiment on the battle fields of Sicily, Italy and Germany and have added proud laurels to your Colours. God Bless you all." Those were stirring words, but the ten battle honours that were soon added to the Regimental Colour had been won at a high price: 264 Patricias killed in action or dead on active service, 1,118 wounded, and 47 taken prisoner. ∎

[facing page] A soldier of 2 PPCLI receives training in the use of a flame-thrower, one of many new weapons the Battalion obtained from US forces. [CFJIC DND 2K-1142-9]

[facing page, inset] Brigade patch for the 25th Canadian Infantry Brigade. [RHK]

[facing page, background] Winter in Korea. [CFJIC DND ZK-2011-6]

1946-1953

Brigadier J.M. Rockingham, commander of the 25th Canadian Infantry Brigade, briefs newly arrived officers of A and C Company, 1 PPCLI, about the enemy situation before they move up into the line to replace C and D Company, 2 PPCLI, Korea, September 1951. From left to right are Captain Jeff Costeloe, Second Lieutenant Val Rithaler, Rockingham, Captain Gord Gunton; behind Gunton is Second Lieutenant Rick Caesar; in front of Gunton is Major Bob Cross; to the left rear of Cross is Captain Lloyd Swick; beside Cross and hidden by the windshield is Major Jeff Williams.

[background] Winter in Korea.
[CFJIC DND ZK-2011-6]

[above] Major George A. Flint briefs patrol leader Sergeant Tommy Prince, a Second World War veteran of the 1st Special Service Force and one of Canada's most decorated aboriginal soldiers. From left to right are Private J.A.R. Chartrand, Prince, Flint, Lieutenant John Deegan and Lieutenant Jack Reagan; to the rear, holding binoculars, is the Company Sergeant Major, Warrant Officer 2nd Class D.H. Acton.

The Early Cold War and the War in Korea

When post-war plans for Canada's military were announced in 1946, the size of the Active Force Army was set at twenty-five thousand, with just seven thousand in the combat arms. Once again, mirroring the inter-war years, the infantry would revert to just three units: Princess Patricia's Canadian Light Infantry, the Royal Canadian Regiment, and the Royal 22nd Regiment. Lieutenant-Colonel Ware resumed command of the peacetime Patricias in early January 1946 and prepared them for their move to a new base at Currie Barracks, on the southwest edge of Calgary, in the spring of that year.

Ware was determined that his Regiment would remain operationally oriented and he focused on Arctic and cold-weather training. Learning how to fight in the north, he reasoned, would not only allow his soldiers to contribute to the potential defence of the nation, but would also provide them with tough physical and mental challenges. In late August 1946, for example, he took the Patricias up the Alaska Highway for an experience that combined scouting out the north while living and training in remote country. As Ware later recorded, "[the exercise] was worth its weight in gold; from it stemmed both winter and summer training policies in the Northwest which became part of Regimental training in the years to come." This exercise prepared the unit for participation in a major Canadian-US exercise called SWEETBRIAR the following February, in which more than five thousand troops from the two countries gathered along the Alaska Highway for winter training.

Ware's plan fitted perfectly with Canada's early Cold War defence policy, which aimed, among other things, to guard the Canadian north against a surprise Soviet attack. The fear that the Russians might try to seize selected areas in Canada's far north might seem like fantasy today, but very little was known about Soviet intentions in the late 1940s. To counter such a possibility, in 1948 the government created the Mobile Striking Force (MSF) — an airborne brigade consisting of all three of the Active Force regiments. In the event of a Soviet landing in the Canadian north, the MSF's mission was to deploy by parachute to the area of concern and form a cohesive defensive force to hold the Soviets while reinforcements arrived overland from southern Canada or the United States.

The Patricias began their parachute training at the Canadian Joint Air Training Centre at Rivers, Manitoba, in late summer 1948. Their conversion from infantry to airborne paratroopers called for specialized training for the men, both as individuals and as members of a fighting team. But the parachute wings that successful volunteers — and most were successful — sported on their uniforms afterward brought added allure to service with the PPCLI. That, and the increased pay and better living conditions that came with the first post-war increase in the defence budget, brought more and higher-quality recruits into Patricia ranks. At the same time, everyone bent to the task of creating a viable airborne capability; all were determined to qualify for the jump wings and pass the initiation together. Thus, another distinctive element was added to the Patricias' tradition.

The Patricias of early 1950 were as well trained a professional peacetime military force as Canada had ever had, but were they ready for the real thing? They would shortly find out. In the pre-dawn hours of June 25, 135,000 troops from communist North Korea, supported by Soviet military advisors and Soviet-built tanks and aircraft, attacked across the 38th parallel — the boundary between the communist North and non-communist South Korea — in a surprise attack that quickly pushed the South's forces into headlong retreat. Suddenly, a new war loomed for Canada.

The United States, strongly supported by the United Kingdom, was determined to stop the invasion. Other members of the North Atlantic Treaty Organization (NATO), newly formed the previous summer, equally believed that, if the invasion were successful, a Soviet attack on western Europe might follow. Taking its case to the United Nations Security Council, the United States persuaded that body to call on all UN member states to come to South Korea's aid and to place their forces under the US commander on the spot, General Douglas MacArthur. Accordingly on August 7, 1950, Canadian Prime Minister Louis St. Laurent announced that Canada would send a brigade group to Korea in response to the UN's call.

In fact, however, Canada had no brigade group to send. Instead, it was decided to form one from newly recruited second battalions. It was hoped that enough veterans might be willing to volunteer for these new units so that their training might be curtailed and the brigade sent to Korea as quickly as possible. Initially known as the Canadian Army Special Force, the formation was soon designated the 25th Canadian Infantry Brigade Group and would be commanded by John Rockingham, who had led such a force successfully during the latter part of the Second World War.

Thus the 2nd Battalion of the PPCLI, known as 2 PPCLI, was formed at Calgary from volunteer veterans, trained at Calgary and Camp Wainwright by the Active Force 1st Battalion, and stiffened by a number of officers and senior NCOs from the Active Force. Rockingham picked Jim Stone to command 2 PPCLI. Physically and mentally tough, Stone had won a Military Cross and a Distinguished Service Order before taking command of the Loyal Edmonton Regiment in Italy, and thus knew the PPCLI well. He was a strict disciplinarian who drove his men hard and insisted that they be in superb physical shape for the upcoming battle.

The tough paratroopers of the 1st Battalion, though, were not particularly happy with their new role. Mel Canfield enlisted in Vancouver on August 13, 1950, and was soon shipped to Calgary to begin training. There, he met the smartly uniformed soldiers of

[top left] Original parachute wings. [RHK]

[top right, l to r] Brigadier B.A. Burke, DSO, Commander, 27th British Commonwealth Brigade, confers with Lieutenant-Colonel Jim Stone, DSO, MC, Commanding Officer, 2 PPCLI.

the 1st Battalion: "They were all so magnificent; jump boots and pressed trousers and pressed shirts and they were angry because we were going to be trained to go to Korea and they were going to have to stay behind. So we didn't get treated too well to start with." On one occasion, Charles Scot-Brown watched a soldier from the 1st Battalion try to prepare a small knot of Second World War veterans for their required Tests of Elementary Training. As Scot-Brown recalled, one of the veterans piped up, "'Never mind all that shit, Corporal, we know all about that. Just show us where

[top left] Soldiers of 2 PPCLI receive letters from home:
(l to r) privates W.R. Disbato, V.C. Bostock, Henry Staples
(holding letter), and M. Kawanami.

[bottom left] Patricias in a slit trench, Korea, early February 1951.

[top right] Captain P.M. Pyne and Private R.G. White,
2 PPCLI, control mortar fire, Korea, 1951.

[bottom right] Privates Bill Boshman and Art Cassidy,
2 PPCLI, man a Bren gun, March 1951. [LAC/DND PA-128817]

[background: CFJIC DND ZK-2011-6]

we got to go and we're all ready to go.'" The corporal stopped his demonstration and told the men, "'Well, soldier, I'm quite sure you do know it, but I'm being paid to make sure you do know it, so I'm going to make sure that you're going to pass your [tests], or you're going to get the training, because I don't want to be responsible for your deaths.'"

The recruiting and training continued through August and September. Then, when the cold weather set in, the PPCLI moved to Fort Lewis, a sprawling US Army base near Seattle, to continue its preparations. Other Canadian units soon followed. By November, it was determined that there were so many volunteers that third battalions could also be formed and held in Canada just in case the war in Korea should go on longer than expected.

In Korea, meanwhile, the communist forces had pushed the South Koreans into a small perimeter around the port of Pusan (now Busan). But General MacArthur had a bold plan to reverse the entire momentum of the war. On November 15, the 1st US Marine Division attacked and captured the small port of Inchon, southwest of Seoul, and pushed inland. Suddenly in danger of being cut off completely, the communists quickly retreated. MacArthur's forces pushed them back across the 38th parallel and drove north almost as far as the Yalu River, marking the border between North Korea and China, whose newly installed communist government warned it would intervene if UN forces came any closer.

With the North Koreans facing imminent defeat, Ottawa believed that a Canadian brigade might not be needed in Korea after all and was anxious to send it instead to Europe as Canada's contribution to NATO. But the United States urged Canada to send at least one battalion to help with occupation duties. The Canadians picked 2 PPCLI as the most ready to go, and Stone and his battalion sailed from Seattle on November 25, 1950, landing in Pusan twenty-four days later.

The South Korea that greeted them was a far cry from the bustling, dynamic, and highly modern country of today. As one Patricia would later recall, "As our troop ship...neared the southern shore of Korea on a dreary, drizzly day we stood lining the rails, wondering what lay ahead of us.... The mystique was soon to disappear when we got our first whiff of the place. A strong smell of sewage struck our nostrils. Welcome to the land of 'Honey Wagons,' night soil, soft coal fires and the stench of too many people crammed into the refugee-filled and overcrowded city." The mayor of Pusan welcomed Stone on behalf of the Korean people while a military band blared out "If I Knew You Were Coming I'd Have Baked a Cake," which they played for every arriving troopship. After four hours of unloading men and supplies, the battalion was trucked to the small island of Mok-to, at the entrance to Pusan harbour. This was to be their base and quarters until they could move inland to finish their combat training.

A Company, 2 PPCLI, advancing along a riverbank, Korea, March 11, 1951. [LAC/DND PA-114888]

[left] Soldiers of 2 PPCLI gather around a stove to keep warm and enjoy a mug of coffee.

[centre] 2 PPCLI Regimental Sergeant Major, Warrant Officer 1st Class Les "Daddy" Grimes.

[right] Soldiers of 2 PPCLI wash up in a stream, Korea, May 1951.

[background: CFJIC DND ZK-2011-6]

[left] Private J. Hoskins, A Company, 2 PPCLI, during the advance to Hill 419, February 1951.

[right] Funeral of the Regimental Sergeant Major of 2 PPCLI, Warrant Officer 1st Class J.D. Woods, DCM, killed in a tragic training accident on January 18, 1951.

While the Patricias were en route to Korea, Chinese "volunteers" infiltrated across the frozen Yalu River border into North Korea and attacked MacArthur's forces on both sides of the peninsula. The UN troops were shocked and surprised by the sudden appearance of hundreds of thousands of Chinese soldiers and quickly retreated. Once again South Korea was in danger of communist envelopment, and MacArthur was desperate to send every available man to the front to stem the Chinese advance. Lieutenant-General Walton H. "Bulldog" Walker, commanding the US Eighth Army, insisted the Patricias move to the front immediately, but Stone strongly dissented. He knew

his troops needed at least six weeks more training before they would be ready for action.

Stone met Walker on December 21 and explained that he had instructions from the Canadian government to refuse a direct order that, in his view, would endanger the very existence of his unit. Walker relented, and the Patricias moved to Miryang, in the mountains, where they trained, absorbed American equipment such as bazookas and 75mm recoilless rifles, and sent home men who were not physically or mentally ready for real war. Then, in mid-February, they were shipped to the front and placed in the 27th British Commonwealth Infantry Brigade (27 BCIB), consisting of 2 PPCLI; 3rd Battalion, The Royal Australian Regiment; 1st Battalion, The Middlesex Regiment (British Army); 1st Battalion, Argyll and

Patricias advance north from Miryang, Korea, in operations as part of the 27th British Commonwealth Brigade, March 1951. [LAC/DND PA-114889]

[top right] A Company, 2 PPCLI, moving along a dyke during a training exercise in the Miryang area, Korea, February 1951.

[centre right] A Company, 2 PPCLI, passing through B Company and heading into action for the first time, Chum Hi Valley, Korea, February 1951. Note that later on the bedrolls and sleeping bags were withdrawn after the Patricias discovered 168 US soldiers killed while trapped in theirs.

[bottom left] A Company, 2 PPCLI, on the march along a paddy field dyke, Korea, March 11, 1951. [LAC/DND PA-114892]

Sutherland Highlanders (British Army); 16th Field Regiment, Royal New Zealand Artillery; and 60th Indian Field Ambulance; and supported by US artillery and the US 72nd Tank Battalion. The Patricias would join the rest of the Canadian brigade when it arrived from Fort Lewis.

On February 21, 1951, the new UN commander, General Matthew Ridgway, replacing the fired MacArthur, launched a major attack all along the front and began to push the Chinese back slowly but steadily, killing large numbers of the enemy with massive artillery barrages and heavy air strikes. The Chinese fought back, mostly at night in mass attacks, but UN firepower was overwhelming, and eventually they withdrew from contact to prepare what would be their last major counterattack of the war.

The Chinese launched their attack before midnight on April 21, their aim to encircle and capture Seoul in a two-pronged assault. One prong was aimed at a South Korean formation, the 6th Republic of Korea Division, holding the line about twenty-five kilometres north of 27 BCIB, which was in reserve near the junction of the Kapyong and Somok-tong rivers. The South Koreans broke, and the brigade found itself the only UN formation standing between the onrushing Chinese and Seoul. The commander, Brigadier B.A. Burke, assigned the Australians and the US tank battalion to defend Hill 504, to the east of the river valley, and the Patricias to defend Hill 677 to the west. Stone studied every possible approach to Hill 677 and prepared his

defences accordingly. Just after midnight on April 23, the Chinese hit the Americans and Australians. The fighting raged through the night and into the day, and by mid-afternoon Burke ordered the heavily pressed forces to withdraw. Then, a few hours later, the Chinese turned their attention to the Patricias. One sergeant later recalled the moment: "They were on top of our positions before we knew it. They're quiet as mice with those rubber shoes of theirs and then there's a whistle. They get up with a shout about [ten] feet from our positions and come in. The first wave throws its grenades, fires its weapons, and goes to the ground. It is followed by a second, which does the same, and then a third comes up. They just keep coming."

The Patricia defences on the eastern and southern slopes of Hill 677 bore the brunt of the early attacks. B Company was almost enveloped while some five hundred Chinese attacked Stone's tactical headquarters. There, four half-tracked vehicles, commanded by Lieutenant Hub Gray and armed with both .30- and .50-calibre machine guns, made short work of them. Just after midnight, though, the Chinese came on again, this time attacking the D company positions. They penetrated the D Company perimeter forcing the company to make a daring decision. They requested that artillery fire be delivered onto their position. The shells came rumbling in, and shrapnel cut the Chinese down by the score while the Patricias hunkered down. The 27 BCIB war diary records that the shelling "was completely successful inflicting heavy

Text visible on the colour:

KAPYONG, KOREA

YPRES 1915 17
MOUNT SORREL
VIMY 1917
AMIENS
PURSUIT TO MONS
LANDING IN SICILY
THE MORO
HITLER LINE
RIMINI LINE
FOSSO MUNIO
KAPYONG

FREZENBERG
FLERS-COURCELETTE
PASSCHENDAELE
SCARPE 1918
FRANCE AND FLANDERS 1914-18
LEONFORTE
THE GULLY
GOTHIC LINE
SAN FORTUNATO
NORTH WEST EUROPE
KOREA

PRINCESS PATRICIA'S CANADIAN LIGHT INFANTRY

[top] 2 PPCLI Regimental Colour with Kapyong streamer.

[bottom] Kapyong memorial, erected as part of the twenty-fifth anniversary celebration of the battle.

[background: CFJIC DND ZK-2011-6]

PPCLI

The Chinese Attack D Company at Kapyong

"The charging Chinese make one hell of a lot of noise, banging bamboo sticks together, rattling noise makers and shouting… As they come forward our booby traps are exploding. Our Vickers machine gun begins to fire but does not last long. Mortars rain down in front of us and there is one hell of a lot of noise. I am scared. The Chinese…begin to infiltrate right into our position. I remember looking at the Bren gunner. He takes a direct hit in the head. His face is smashed to hell, contorted blood and mashed flesh — it literally disintegrates in front of my face. I can't remember anything after that."

with the battalion and at all times by veterans of the battle.

In the next few months, the rest of the Canadian brigade group arrived, and the 1st Commonwealth Division — consisting of a British brigade, a mixed British Commonwealth brigade, the Canadian brigade, and other troops — was formed as the UN slowly pushed the Chinese back to positions dubbed the Jamestown Line, straddling the 38th parallel. Truce talks began and dragged on for nearly two years, with the two sides restricting themselves to actions along the Jamestown Line for the duration of the war. Thus, for the Patricias, as for the rest of the Canadians, the Korean War after the start of the peace talks meant patrolling no man's land and defending against company-size attacks at night, and occasional forays against the enemy's lines. It was also a war of boredom, extreme cold in the winter, extreme heat in the summer, illness, and irrelevance. The original Special Force volunteers in 2 PPCLI rotated back to Canada beginning in mid-October 1951 and were replaced by the paratroopers of the 1st Battalion under the command of Lieutenant-Colonel Norman Wilson-Smith, and Lieutenant-Colonel J.R. Cameron, successively.

Their war was very different from the battles fought by 2 PPCLI. On the night of December 10/11, 1951, for

enemy casualties and daylight found the D Company still in position and holding their ground."

By dawn, the Chinese pulled back, and the Patricias were isolated atop the hill and needed to be resupplied by air. They had lost ten killed and twenty-three wounded, but they had held the enemy and allowed UN troops farther south to consolidate their lines and begin to push the Chinese back. For their valour, most of the units of the brigade, including 2 PPCLI, were later awarded the highly regarded United States Presidential Unit Citation, a blue streamer affixed to the 2nd Battalion's Colour to this day. The emblem for the citation is worn on the sleeves of members serving

example, D Company, 1 PPCLI, was ordered to take three Chinese-held hills across from the Canadian positions. Supported by the 2nd Regiment, Royal Canadian Horse Artillery, a troop of Strathcona tanks, and British and Royal 22nd Regiment mortars, the Patricias left their positions atop Hill 227 at about ten p.m. under a clear sky and a bright moon. Two platoons worked their way forward in line abreast with no opposition until 11 Platoon on the right reached a ridge between two of the three hills. Here, it was grenaded and shelled. The Strathconas moved up and engaged the enemy positions with direct fire, silencing them. On the left, the Chinese defenders opened rifle and machine-gun fire on 12 Platoon. The Patricias took a dozen casualties before the platoon was forced to withdraw. The company commander, Major J.H.B. George, was wounded at about that time, and his communications were cut when the radio was hit by a Chinese bullet, but he still led a renewed attack by 11 Platoon, which, after four tries, took the most easterly hill. 10 Platoon, held in reserve until then, now joined the fight and captured the saddle between the objective and Hill 227. No prisoners were taken in the raid, in which one Patricia was killed and twenty-four wounded. Major George was awarded the Distinguished Service Order for his leadership in this short clash.

By the fall of 1952, both the UN and the communists were sending patrols out night after night. The Chinese usually sent larger parties than the Canadians, but the Canadians could often rely on registered artillery or tank fire for support if they ran into difficulties. Sometimes, there were no clashes between the opposing forces. At other times, the fighting in the dark, somewhere near the Samichon River, was both vicious and deadly.

One night in early October, Sergeant John Richardson was leading a "standing" patrol mounted by 12 Platoon, D Company of 1 PPCLI. (A "standing patrol" is a listening post, established after dark, forward of the main defensive positions, to determine what the enemy is up to.) Richardson heard Chinese digging and decided to call down artillery fire on the approximate position of the noise. He reached for his signaller's microphone. "Just then," he later recalled, "a shadowy form came towards us and I reckoned it was one of ours. 'Where the hell do you think you're going?'" Richardson called out. That was a mistake. "It turned out he was a scout for the … enemy patrol and he couldn't get his burp gun in action." Shooting broke out immediately. The Patricia signaller's radio was shot off his back as the Chinese soldier disappeared into the night. Bren gunner Private C.H. Chute opened fire, shooting many Chinese, but Lance Corporal Johnstone was killed by small-arms fire. The Patricia patrol was outnumbered and outgunned. Richardson and two other men, Sergeant Rocky Prentice and Corporal D.P. Hastings, armed with two US rapid-fire carbines and a Tommy gun, provided covering fire for the rest of the patrol as Chute led them into a defensive

Major E.D. "Oop" MacPhail, C Company, 3 PPCLI, and Major Bill Little, Lord Strathcona's Horse, check out the area of the Hook, Korea, 1953.

bleeding away of Chinese lives, and threats that the new US president, Dwight D. Eisenhower, would use nuclear weapons to end the war, the communists finally agreed to an armistice on July 27, 1953. By then, the three battalions of the PPCLI had sent an estimated 3,800 soldiers to Korea, of whom 537 had become casualties: 107 killed in action, 429 wounded, and 1 taken prisoner. In total, 21,940 Canadian soldiers served in Korea. Of these, 309 were killed in action, died of wounds, or are still missing and presumed to have been killed; 1,251 were wounded; and 32 became prisoners of war. An additional 93 soldiers and sailors were dead from non-battle causes.

Korea remains divided. Cynics might say that the deaths of the Patricias and those of the many other UN soldiers from South Korea, the United States, Britain, Australia, and dozens of other countries that came to South Korea's aid were in vain. But South Korea today is a thriving and prosperous democracy while its northern cousin starves under a repressive and closed regime. In one way, then, the West's victory in the Cold War began in the frozen hills of Korea. And, once again, Hamilton Gault's Regiment played a proud and honourable part. ∎

circle on a nearby knoll. Then Hastings was killed, Prentice took a bullet in the hip, and Richardson was hit with grenade fragments. Richardson and Prentice were barely able to crawl toward the other men. Led by Corporal Pahall, the survivors edged slowly out of the area as friendly artillery fire began to explode in the vicinity of the Chinese. Eventually, the patrol survivors met a rescue party that had come forward from the line. For their bravery in trying to cover the withdrawal of their men that night, Richardson was awarded a Distinguished Conduct Medal and Prentice the Military Medal.

The 3rd Battalion relieved 1 PPCLI on November 3, 1952, and took over its positions on the Jamestown Line, holding them as the war dragged on through the spring and into the summer of 1953. With the death of Soviet dictator Josef Stalin earlier in the year, the constant

[facing page] Corporal Calvin Berube, C Company, 1 PPCLI, alongside his LAV III, during Exercise PHOENIX RAM, Wainwright, Alberta, 2005. [CFJIC DND LV2005-A040]

[facing page, inset] Olive Drab Cloth Cap Badge. [RHK]

1954-2013

[top] The Regiment, reconstituted as Princess Patricia's Canadian Light Infantry of the Active Force, arrives at Currie Barracks, Calgary, June 1946.

[centre] Brass belt buckle. [RHK]

[bottom] Corporal R. Anderson, who, as a member of the 1st Canadian Parachute Battalion, participated in the seizure of the Dives Crossing Bridge on D-Day, June 5/6, 1944, prepares in mid-1960 to make his last parachute drop as Jumpmaster Sergeant Bill Harris does a final check. [CFJIC DND WES66-27]

[background] 1 PPCLI training, 1985.

On Guard in Europe and at Home

The Patricias returned to Canada from Korea with a new mandate: preserving peace at home and around the world. Uneasy relations with the Soviet Union created a "cold" war unlike anything Canada had ever known. Led by the United States, the Western democracies had formed NATO in 1949 to deter Soviet aggression in Europe and elsewhere. NATO was Canada's first peacetime military alliance, and Canada was obliged by the treaty to make land, air, and sea contributions to the common defence. After Korea, then, there were no deep and rapid cuts to the Canadian defence budget as there had been after the First and Second World Wars. Rather, Canada, along with almost all the other NATO countries, launched the largest peacetime mobilization in its history. In 1950 the entire Canadian Armed Forces — land, sea, and air — had numbered forty thousand; by 1955 the Force had expanded to one hundred forty thousand.

As one of the Canadian Army's three Active Force infantry regiments, the PPCLI was directly affected by the rapid growth in Canadian military capability. Although the 3rd Battalion was reduced to "nil strength" in January 1954 (meaning it continued to officially exist but with no troops), the 2nd Battalion underwent parachute training after its return from Korea and was then dispatched for a two-year posting to Canada's NATO brigade in Germany. When 2 PPCLI returned from Europe, it was initially stationed in Currie Barracks, Calgary, before being relocated a year and a

The M113 Armoured Personnel Carrier

Major Charles "Chic" Goodman commanded the first Patricia company to be equipped with M113 Armoured Personnel Carriers, in 1965. He later recalled: "It was a real treat to train with these and have them on the exercise…. We drove them up the Autobahn, from Fort MacLeod in Hemer, Germany, to the training area at Soltau. It must have terrified every German on the Autobahn as these things came hurtling down. We didn't know enough at the time not to drive them flat out…that it was going to shorten the track life of these things."

Major "Chic" Goodman, C Company, 1 PPCLI, with a newly arrived M113 armoured personnel carrier, Haltern training area, West Germany, 1965.

half later to the newly constructed Hamilton Gault Barracks at Greisbach, Alberta, outside of Edmonton. Eventually it was relocated to the Kapyong Barracks in Winnipeg, and then finally to Canadian Armed Forces Base (CFB) Shilo, near Brandon, Manitoba. 2 PPCLI was relieved in Germany by the 1st Battalion, which returned to Canada in 1957 to occupy Work Point Barracks near Victoria, BC. Patricia battalions returned to Germany several times before Canada withdrew its ground troops from that country in 1993, after the end of the Cold War.

In the first decade and a half of their nearly forty years in post-war Europe, Canadian soldiers trained to operate with a full range of modern equipment, including tactical nuclear weapons mounted on short-range missiles. The British-built Centurion tanks of the Royal Canadian Armoured Corps were first class. So were the US-built M113 armoured personnel carriers, which the Canadian Army first deployed in Europe in 1965. Until then, Canadian infantry in Germany had been motorized, but the M113 — designed to carry infantry into battle alongside the armour — increased the infantry's tempo and flexibility, the essence of its new mechanized role. Year in and year out, Patricias and other Canadian units practised for a high-level war to defend western Europe from the Soviet-led Warsaw Pact countries. The Patricias' role was to fight as members of combined arms teams with Canada's armour to stop Soviet armour from overwhelming NATO and buy time for reinforcements to arrive from Britain and North America.

[top right] Sergeant Major Jack Rudd chats with Patricias of 1 PPCLI as they board a C-119 "Flying Boxcar" rigged for deployment by parachute to the exercise BULLDOG IV, 1955. [LAC/DND PL-76871]

[bottom right] A patrol of Patricias in a winter exercise, possibly in the foothills of northern Alberta; the patrol leader carries a Sten gun and the number two a Bren gun.

Canada's brigade in Europe was initially designated the 27th Canadian Infantry Brigade Group; later it became the 4th Canadian Infantry Brigade Group, and finally, in 1958, the 4th Canadian Mechanized Brigade Group. Initially, the brigade was stationed on the North German Plain with the British Army of the Rhine, and it was there that the Patricia battalions completed four tours of duty. In the early 1970s, the brigade moved south to Baden-Württemberg to serve as NATO's strategic reserve; 2 PPCLI served one tour of duty in that location.

Vastly outnumbered by the tank and heavy-armour formations of the Warsaw Pact, the NATO forces had to undertake demanding and intensive training, frequently conducted — in a first for the Patricias — on ground over which they intended to fight. Indeed, training alongside allies, in a realistic setting, to fight an opponent who was well defined and close at hand gave "soldiering" a certain edge that was perhaps not always possible for Canadian-based battalions. During the years the Regiment served in Germany, the training cycle was carefully and predictably designed, largely because managing the movement of troops in heavily populated areas required considerable coordination. In the north and south of Germany, the Patricias focused their training on rapid, efficient deployment drills, mobile defence, and hasty and deliberate counterattacks. Many a Patricia looks back on NATO service in Germany with

[top left] Soldiers of 1 PPCLI "cam up" during Exercise WAINCON, Wainwright, Alberta, 1978.

[top right] A soldier of 3 PPCLI Reconnaissance Platoon.

[bottom left] Patricias of the 3rd Battalion exit their Grizzly armoured personnel carrier during an exercise in Suffield, Alberta, 1981.

[facing page, top] Soldiers of 9 Platoon, C Company, 1 PPCLI, camouflaged and ready for deployment, Exercise WAINCON, Wainwright, Alberta, 1978.

[facing page, bottom] 1 PPCLI crossing Ribstone Creek, Wainwright, Alberta, 1985.

[background] Soldiers of 1 PPCLI advance using fire and movement across an open field in Wainwright, Alberta, during Exercise RENDEZVOUS, 1989.

nostalgia, not only for the unique experience — soldiers and their families saw a posting to Germany as a stroke of good fortune — but also for the chance to train within large formations, a chance that seemed lost forever when Canada pulled out of its NATO standing force commitment in 1993. And although exercises conducted in populated areas occasionally restricted manoeuvres, the variety of terrain provided by Germany's villages, towns, and carefully manicured woods and fields provided an added realistic dimension to training that could not be replicated in Canada.

For the Canadian-based battalions, training might have lacked the immediacy and geographic unique-ness of a German deployment, but the Regiment's characteristic professional tempo and focus were no less apparent. In Canada, field training was most often conducted on the sprawling ranges and man-oeuvre areas of the Wainwright, Shilo, and Dundurn (Saskatchewan) training grounds, which still provide firing and exercise opportunities that are the envy of other armies and far superior to training opportun-ities in Europe. Training in Canada followed its own intensive cycle, with field exercises in the fall followed by unit-run junior leadership, support weapons, and drivers' courses, and winter indoctrination training. Christmas leave was almost always followed by a taxing cold weather exercise, another set of specialty weapons and trades courses, and, in the spring work-up, field train-ing that culminated in a six-week brigade- or army-level concentra-tion. For Patricia battalions based in Canada, the months from September to mid-May almost always passed in a purpose-ful blur of activity.

Battalion life in Canada during the Cold War was always busy and demanding; and although the general structure of the training year was virtually constant, there was more than sufficient variety and imagina-tion in the design and conduct of exercises to ensure that the units and their leaders were trained to a high degree of general readiness. But in addition to the annual Canadian-based training cycle, PPCLI bat-talions routinely punctuated the year with adventure training, small-unit exchanges, mountain warfare and survival skills courses, patrol schools, peacekeeping tours in Cyprus, assistance to the civil authority in fighting floods and forest fires, exercises in the high arctic in winter, and occasional flyovers to train in northern Norway. It was a challenging and stressful lifestyle that saw the Regiment's members spending much more time away than at home. But it resulted in the formation of capable, experienced, well-rounded, flexible, and superbly trained units and individuals.

In September 1953, Lady Patricia Ramsay visited her 2nd Battalion at Currie Barracks near Calgary to present the Queen's and Regimental Colours.

On that occasion, for the first time, the Regimental Colour carried the Patricias' Second World War and Korean War Battle Honours. On the fiftieth anniversary of the Regiment in 1964, Lady Patricia visited her 1st Battalion in Germany and her 2nd Battalion in Edmonton to repeat the ceremonies she had first performed at Bramshott in 1919, placing a silver gilt wreath of laurel on the Regimental Colour. She was still Colonel-in-Chief of the Patricias when she died on January 12, 1974. She was succeeded by her cousin, Patricia Edwina Victoria Mountbatten — Lady Brabourne — who filled Lady Patricia's shoes most successfully with many trips to her Regiment both in Canada and occasionally in the field and on peacekeeping deployments. She retired in early 2007 and was replaced as Colonel-in-Chief by the Right Honourable Adrienne Clarkson, former governor general of Canada.

[top left] The Colonel-in-Chief, Lady Patricia, presents a replica of the Wreath of Laurel to the 1st Battalion during the celebration of the Regiment's fiftieth anniversary, Fort MacLeod, Deilinghofen, West Germany, August 10, 1964, witnessed by the Colonel of the Regiment, Major-General Ware, and the Commanding Officer, Lieutenant-Colonel George Brown; the Colour Officer is Second Lieutenant Merv McMurray.

[top right] Her Majesty Queen Elizabeth II presents new Colours, emblazoned with Second World War Battle Honours, to the 1st Battalion in Beacon Hill Park, Victoria, July 17, 1959. The kneeling subaltern for the new Queen's Colour is Lieutenant Mel Canfield, a Kapyong veteran.

[facing page] 1 Canadian Mechanized Brigade Group shoulder patch. [RHK]

[top left] The Colonel-in-Chief, Lady Patricia Brabourne, and Colonel R. Stone, Commanding Officer of 2 PPCLI at Kapyong, stand on the dais at the Winnipeg Convention Centre during the twenty-fifth anniversary of the Battle of Kapyong, March 26, 1976. Sergeant V.B. (Rick) Hillyard, a Kapyong veteran, reads the United States Presidential Unit Citation awarded to 2 PPCLI for its stand at Kapyong, Korea, 1951.

[top right] The Old Guard during the Regiment's eightieth anniversary, Currie Barracks, Calgary, 1994.

[centre left] The recently designated 3rd Battalion, PPCLI, receives its first set of Colours on November 20, 1971, from Governor General Roland Michener at Work Point Barracks, Esquimalt, British Columbia.

[bottom left] 3 PPCLI receives replacement Colours at Pakrac, Croatia, March 17, 1993, the only time in Canadian history that Colours have been presented to a battalion on operational duty. (standing l to r) Major Craig King, Field Officer for the new Regimental Colour; Colonel of the Regiment, Major-General Herb Pitts, MC (saluting); the Colonel-in-Chief, Lady Patricia (saluting); and Major David Barr, Field Officer for the new Queen's Colour. (kneeling, l to r) Lieutenant Chris Ankerson, Subaltern for the new Regimental Colour; and Lieutenant Mike Gagné, Subaltern for the new Queen's Colour.

[facing page] 4 Canadian Mechanized Brigade Group shoulder patch. [RHK]

The Regimental Colours have evolved to reflect changing times in the Regiment. In June 1956, the streamer of the United States Presidential Unit Citation was attached to the Colours of 2 PPCLI by Livingstone T. Merchant, US ambassador to Canada. In 1959, Her Majesty the Queen presented the 1st Battalion with its new Colours, while the 3rd Battalion received its first Colours from Governor General Roland Michener on November 20, 1971. In 1993 the Colonel-in-Chief, accompanied by Colonel of the Regiment Major-General Herb Pitts, presented 3 PPCLI with new Colours in Pakrac, Croatia, the first time in the Regiment's history that the ceremony had ever taken place in an operational theatre.

When the 3rd Battalion was reduced to nil strength in early 1954, many of the officers and men were transferred to the 2nd Battalion of the newly created Canadian Guards. When Canada's defence budget was cut in the late 1960s and early 1970s, this Regiment, and several others, were either eliminated or became reserve units. One of the units transferred to the reserves was the Queen's Own Rifles of Canada, which had sent battalions to fight in both World Wars. When the 2nd Battalion of the Queen's Own, based in Calgary, was disbanded, many of its members transferred to the Patricias. The transition went smoothly. One former Queen's Own Rifles officer who made the change of regimental affiliation was Major-General Lewis MacKenzie: "When it was announced that the Queen's Own was reduced to nil strength, as were the Black Watch and the Guards, there was no hesitation whatsoever in all of the [2nd Battalion of the] Queen's Own…that we would rebadge PPCLI, being sort of the Army of the West, and knowing members of the Regiment very well.… [N]obody but nobody could ever say anything other than that the Patricias welcomed the Queen's Own with open arms. It was an unbelievably successful amalgamation." Thus the PPCLI once again had three battalions in the Regular Force. The Loyal Edmonton Regiment, a reserve unit, is affiliated as the 4th Battalion, PPCLI.

Most Canadians paid little attention to their servicemen and women in Europe. After all, there was no shooting war there, and few Canadians believed there ever would be. But when floods or fires or civil disorder threatened at home, the Canadian Army was often called upon to help Canadians. Like other units, the Patricias earned plaudits from their fellow Canadians for saving lives and property. This wasn't war against an enemy, but it was war against chaos.

One of the greatest natural disasters to ever challenge a Canadian city was the Manitoba flood of 1950. The Red River of the North rises in the Dakotas and flows north to Lake Winnipeg. When heavy snows fall on the plains states during winter and a slow thaw with major ice jams in the river create a larger than normal flow in the Red, Manitobans brace for spring flooding. By the beginning of May 1950, Manitobans knew they were in for serious flooding as water levels rose in North Dakota and southern Manitoba and the flood crest rolled north to Winnipeg. Over a thousand square kilometres of farmland were transformed into a huge lake. On May 6, Manitoba Premier Douglas Campbell approached Prime Minister Louis St. Laurent with a request to send in the army to help build dikes and evacuate low-lying areas of the city, which lies at the junction of the Red and Assiniboine rivers. The Calgary-based PPCLI was among the first units to get the call. The Patricias worked tirelessly over the next few weeks to contain the flood and help navy and air force personnel and civil authorities to evacuate more than one hundred thousand people — about a third of Winnipeg's entire population. Fighting floods in Manitoba became all too common for the Patricias, who were called upon to help again and again over the years.

In October 1970, two branches of the separatist terrorist Front de Libération du Québec kidnapped the British trade commissioner to Canada in Montreal, James Cross, and Pierre Laporte, a Quebec cabinet minister. They were held for a list of political demands that the Canadian government, headed by Pierre Trudeau, refused to grant. Trudeau invoked the War Measures Act and sent troops to guard vulnerable locations in the province and to support local and Quebec police in protecting prominent individuals. Many of these troops were Quebec based. The Patricias were deployed in Montreal and tasked with protecting the hydro grid which circled the island and later with conducting house searches. The soldiers conducted themselves with calm dignity, and no incidents involving soldiers were ever recorded. Just six years later, the Patricias were again sent to Quebec, but for a much happier occasion: the Games of the XXI Olympiad, the first ever held in Canada, opened in Montreal on July 17, 1976. They were heavily guarded due to the murder of Israeli athletes at the 1972 Olympic Games in Munich. The Patricias, along with thousands of other Canadian troops, helped provincial and local police provide security in and around the Olympic venues.

In spring 1997, Winnipeg was threatened with yet another monster flood. Much of the water was routed past the city by the Red River Floodway, which had been built following the devastating flood of 1950, but dozens of communities both up- and downriver were inundated or left isolated behind flood barriers. Up to the last moment, no one was sure that Winnipeg itself would not succumb. Once again, Ottawa was called on to help the civil authorities, and the Patricias were first on the scene — eventually some eight thousand five hundred troops in total were committed to Manitoba. Troops filled sandbags, shored up dikes, maintained communications networks, and helped evacuate citizens along the river.

In May 2011 it was the Assiniboine, not the Red, that threatened southern Manitoba. Once again the Patricias (the 2nd Battalion, based at CFB Shilo) were called upon to deal with the emergency. The dikes along the river east of Brandon were failing under pressure from the flooded river, and the PPCLI had to shore them up. Virtually no roads led to the area, so some imaginative thinking was needed. C Company filled the bill, as the regimental publication *The Patrician* described events: "Through the innovative use of ATVs, tracked dump trucks, and most notably a small squadron of contracted helicopters, over 1500 sandbags could be placed by 15 soldiers an hour. After the first few days, the Co[mpan]y settled into a predictable, albeit demanding, daily routine consisting of 12 hour workdays."

Forest fires are another natural menace all too common in the park belt north of the Prairies and in British Columbia, and again the Patricias have often helped their fellow western Canadians in time of need. In early August 2003, eighty-five soldiers

[top left] Soldiers of 2 PPCLI participate in flood-control operations on the Red River south of Winnipeg, spring 1974. [CFJIC DND IW74-13]

[top right] Soldiers of 2 PPCLI patrol in front of Stony Mountain Prison, north of Winnipeg, during a strike by guards, 1974.

[bottom right] Master Corporal Leonard Barr patrols the flooded district of Turnbull Drive south of Winnipeg as members of 2PPCLI provide assistance to provincial authorities to counter the flood threat in Manitoba in 1974.

The Rim of the Pacific Exercise (RIMPAC), is the world's largest maritime wartime exercise, featuring fifteen member nations and six observing countries.

[top] The rigorous standard of training the regiment strives to maintain is evident during Exercise RIMPAC. A Company, 1 PPCLI, boards the aircraft carrier U.S.S. *Bonhomme Richard* for amphibious operations, 2008. [CFJIC DND 080710-N-1722M-147]

[centre right] A section of 2 PPCLI participates in a live fire exercise during Exercise RIMPAC, Hawaii, 2012. [CFJIC DND GG2012-0378-008]

[facing page] The PPCLI Regiment continues to train for future clashes and peacekeeping missions. Warrant Officer Robby Fraser directs machine gun fire during a platoon live fire assault at the Pohakuloa training area in Hawaii during Exercise RIMPAC, July 2012. [CFJIC DND 120722-M-VB788-092]

PPCLI soldiers provide critical support roles allowing the front-line firefighters the opportunity to concentrate on emerging or unstable fires. [CFJIC DND IS2003-1291d]

from 1 PPCLI, based in Edmonton, were dispatched to join Operation PEREGRINE, centred on Merritt, British Columbia. The hot summer that year produced hundreds of large and deadly forest fires throughout the province; at the height of the crisis more than eight hundred were burning at any one time. The Patricias received three days of firefighting training before being deployed to the McLure-Barriere region, near Kamloops, where they spent long days building fireguards and mopping up hot spots. After two weeks on the line, the Patricias returned to Edmonton to be relieved by another Canadian Armed Forces unit, but after only six days they were hurriedly sent back to the Kelowna region, where a huge fire threatened the bustling Okanagan city. More than two hundred

fifty homes were destroyed in one firestorm on August 21, 2003. The Patricias stayed and aided in the final mopping up of the fire and construction of fireguards until September 12.

Such natural disaster deployments are regular fare for the Canadian Armed Forces. Flooding, ice storms, extreme blizzards, and the like often require the military's special heavy equipment and communications and organizational skills. But one of the largest domestic deployments ever was to British Columbia for security operations during the 2010 Vancouver Winter Olympics. Dubbed Operation PODIUM, land, sea, and air forces deployed to secure the Olympic venues in and around Vancouver and at Whistler, where major ski events were held. 2 PPCLI set up a wide perimeter around Whistler Village and patrolled the mountains surrounding the resort town. Though rarely seen by the athletes or the spectators, the Patricias maintained constant contact with the various police forces and other security agencies involved. ■

[facing page] Master Corporal Dobson at Camp Claude Berger, Louroujina, Cyprus, named to honour a soldier of the Canadian Airborne Regiment killed during the Turkish invasion in 1974.

[facing page, inset] Non-Commissioned Members (NCM) Collar Badge, 1956-present. [RHK]

[facing page, background] A typical United Nations observation post, Cyprus. [CFJIC DND IWC90-95]

1956-2013

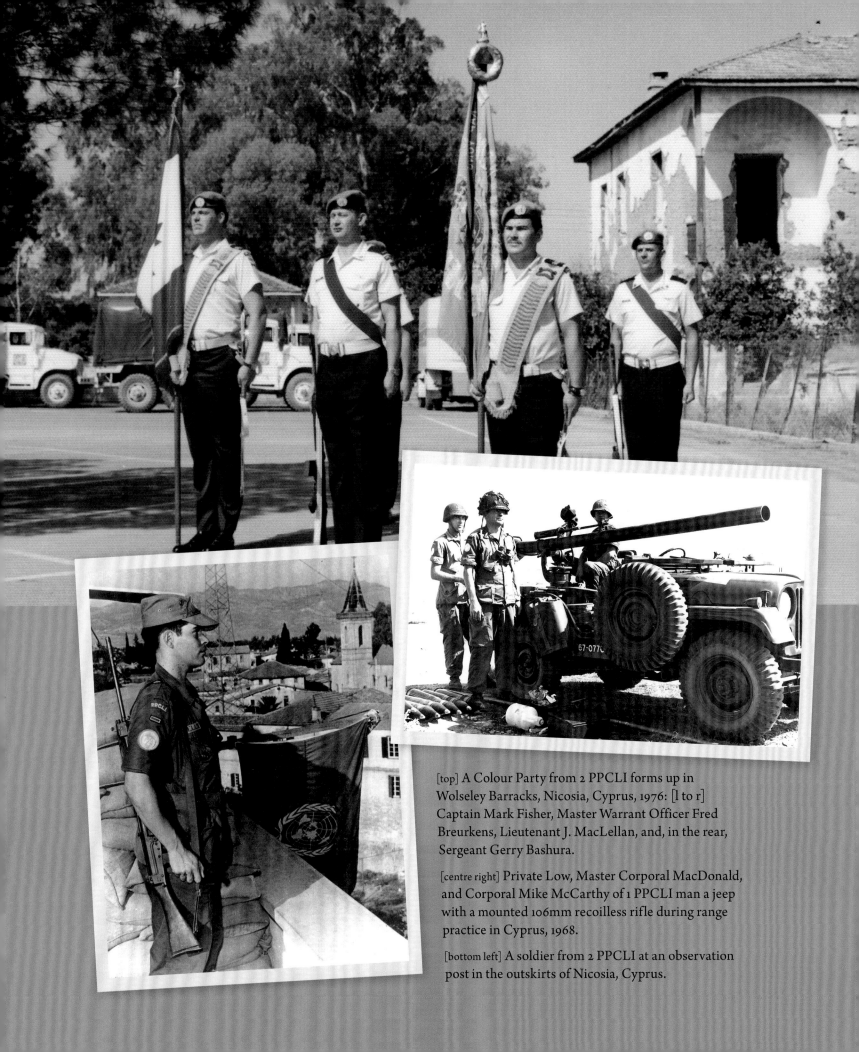

[top] A Colour Party from 2 PPCLI forms up in Wolseley Barracks, Nicosia, Cyprus, 1976: [l to r] Captain Mark Fisher, Master Warrant Officer Fred Breurkens, Lieutenant J. MacLellan, and, in the rear, Sergeant Gerry Bashura.

[centre right] Private Low, Master Corporal MacDonald, and Corporal Mike McCarthy of 1 PPCLI man a jeep with a mounted 106mm recoilless rifle during range practice in Cyprus, 1968.

[bottom left] A soldier from 2 PPCLI at an observation post in the outskirts of Nicosia, Cyprus.

Keeping the Peace

In October 1956, Israel, Britain, and France invaded Egypt in a coordinated attack after the Egyptians nationalized the Suez Canal. Canada's minister of foreign affairs, Lester B. Pearson, came up with a scheme to stop the fighting, get the invaders to withdraw, and possibly move the conflict to the peace table. He proposed that a United Nations Emergency Force (UNEF), a lightly armed UN-directed force, stand between the antagonists to prevent further fighting. Pearson won the Nobel Peace Prize for his "invention" of peacekeeping, and the Canadian Army added this task to its list of important missions. From that time until after the end of the Cold War in the mid-1990s, Canada's military hardly missed a single UN peacekeeping operation.

On Cyprus, for example, fighting erupted between the Greek and Turkish communities shortly after the island gained independence from Britain in 1964. Canada volunteered troops for the UN peacekeeping force for the island, and 1 PPCLI deployed there in April 1968. Eventually all three battalions served there until Canada withdrew in 1991. At first, the Patricias were given responsibility for keeping the peace in the north-central sector of the island; headquarters were in the mountains south of the port of Kyrenia and northeast of the capital of Nicosia. Later deployments were consolidated in Nicosia and its environs. Cyprus was an important mission because both Greece and Turkey were (and still are) NATO members. Keeping the peace on the island not only helped its population; it also lessened the danger that deteriorating

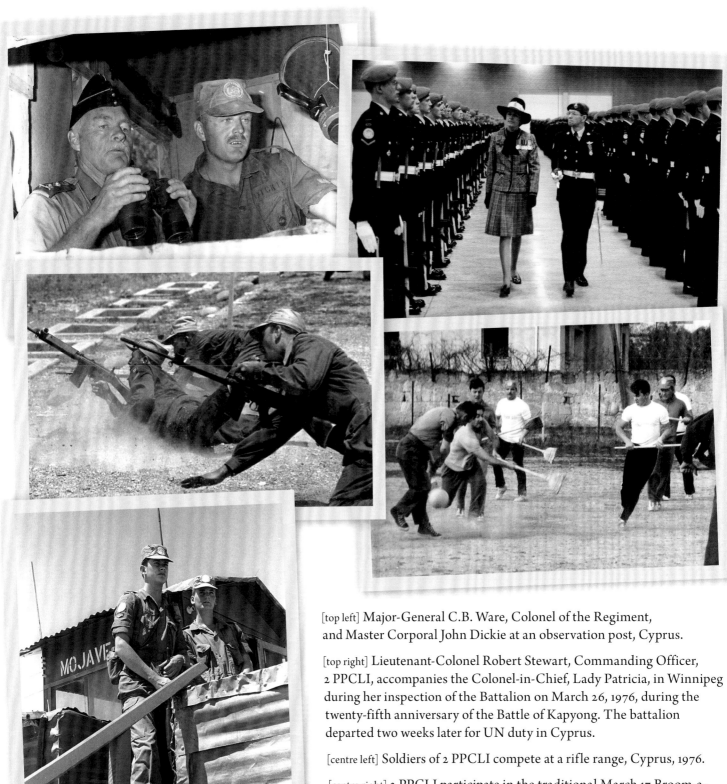

[top left] Major-General C.B. Ware, Colonel of the Regiment, and Master Corporal John Dickie at an observation post, Cyprus.

[top right] Lieutenant-Colonel Robert Stewart, Commanding Officer, 2 PPCLI, accompanies the Colonel-in-Chief, Lady Patricia, in Winnipeg during her inspection of the Battalion on March 26, 1976, during the twenty-fifth anniversary of the Battle of Kapyong. The battalion departed two weeks later for UN duty in Cyprus.

[centre left] Soldiers of 2 PPCLI compete at a rifle range, Cyprus, 1976.

[centre right] 2 PPCLI participate in the traditional March 17 Broom-a-Loo game, Nicosia, Cyprus, 1973.

[bottom left] Patricias from 2 PPCLI man Observation Post Mojave, located in the western suburbs of Nicosia, Cyprus, 1973.
[CFJIC DND IL80-486]

[top] Three Patricias patrol the Green Line between Greek and Turkish sectors of Nicosia, Cyprus. [CFJIC DND ISC84-355]

[centre] A Patricia corporal mans a .50-calibre heavy machine gun on an M113 armoured personnel carrier, Cyprus. [CFJIC DND IL76-328]

[bottom] A Patricia soldier briefs Lady Patricia on the situation at his observation post outside Nicosia, Cyprus. [CFJIC DND ISC84-332]

relations between Greece and Turkey might endanger NATO's southern flank.

That danger suddenly increased greatly in July 1974 when Turkish armed forces suddenly invaded the northern, Turkish-speaking, part of the island. Turkish paratroopers quickly brushed aside the UN peacekeepers and effectively partitioned the island, with the Turkish community forming a self-declared independent republic on the island's northern half. The partition, or Green Line, meandered from Larnaca Bay on the island's southeast coast to Morphou Bay on the northwest coast and cut through the capital.

Cyprus showed both the strengths and the weaknesses of the traditional type of UN "Blue Helmet" peacekeeping operation. In the thirteen rotations that Patricia battalions spent on Cyprus from April 1968 to August 1991, there were many individual shooting incidents between Greek and Turkish Cypriots and some shots even directed at the Canadians. Canadians also helped unearth evidence of mass atrocities that had taken place in the earliest days of the inter-communal conflict. It eventually became apparent that neither the Greek nor the Turkish Cypriots, nor the Turkish Army, which occupied northern Cyprus from July 1974 on, had any intention of breaking the military status quo, and so, with no end in sight to the Cyprus commitment, Canada decided to withdraw.

In June 1991, following the death of communist strongman Josip Tito, Yugoslavia started to break apart. First to go was the far western region of Slovenia, quickly followed by Croatia and Bosnia. Serbia and Montenegro dominated the old Yugoslav government and army, however, and fought to keep the secessions from spreading. But the breakaway regions fought back. Fighting raged, and atrocities and ethnic cleansing broke out in all the conflict areas. The three main religious groups — Serbian Orthodox, Croatian Roman Catholic, and Bosnian Muslim — had a long legacy of mistrust and even hatred. Moderates were ignored; warlords ruled the day.

In January 1992, the UN intervened to establish UNPROFOR (United Nations Protection Force) to separate ethnic Serbs and Croats in Croatia. The first Patricia battalion to serve in Croatia was 3 PPCLI, under the command of Lieutenant-Colonel Glenn W. Nordick, which formed the core of "CANBAT 1," the UN's designation for the Canadian battalion serving with UNPROFOR. Nordick's area of operations was Sector West — the central Krajina region of Croatia. His battalion was augmented by regular soldiers from 2 PPCLI and reserve soldiers from Militia units across Canada but especially from the west. Nordick was shocked by the depth of ethnic hatred between Serbs and Croats, the violence they inflicted on each other, and the atrocities that occurred almost daily.

On April, 4, 1993, the 3 PPCLI battle group was replaced in Sector West by a 2 PPCLI battle group commanded by Lieutenant-Colonel Jim Calvin. At first, the new battle group, roughly 40 per cent of whose augmentees were reserve soldiers, operated under very much the same conditions and in the same area as had its predecessor. Then, on July 5, Calvin was ordered to deploy half his strength to the Peruca Dam area in Sector South, a region of the Krajina known as the Medak Pocket. The battalion remained split between two sectors for approximately six weeks. Sector South, however, was unlike Sector West. In the Medak Pocket, both the Croats and the Serbs were fully armed with tanks and small arms. The perimeter of the sector was defined by dug-in troops, and artillery and tank fire were routine.

On August 26, the UNPROFOR commander decided that 2 PPCLI would replace a French battalion in Sector South permanently, and on September 4 a reunited 2 PPCLI formally assumed responsibility for two thousand four hundred square kilometres of the sector formerly held by the French. Less than a week later, on September 9, the Croatian Army launched an all-out offensive in the Medak Pocket to drive the Serbian forces — and every Serb living

The Colonel of the Regiment, Major-General Pitts, passes the Regimental Colour to Lieutenant Ankerson, Pakrac, Croatia, March 17, 1993. Also visible are the Field Officer for the Regimental Colour, Major King, and the Subaltern for the Queen's Colour, Lieutenant Gagné.

in the area — out of the Krajina. Croatian artillery fire ranged across the Canadian positions. 9 Platoon, commanded by Lieutenant Trevor Greene and located in the village of Medak, received more than five hundred rounds in the first twenty-four hours, and four Canadian soldiers were wounded. Serbian forces retaliated against the Croats by bringing up their own tanks, artillery, and additional troops. The Croatian advance stalled, and both sides dug in around Medak. The Croats then agreed to a UN-brokered ceasefire and a return to the positions they had occupied on September 9, before their offensive had started.

On September 14, the tempo of the Canadians' Medak Operation accelerated when Calvin received formal orders from UNPROFOR headquarters to hold the Serbian forces in their current positions, move the Croatian forces back to the September 9 start line, and establish a UN-controlled buffer zone in the former combat zone. 2 PPCLI was also required to maintain control over the rest of the Canadian area of operations. Calvin expressed his grave concern, however, that the Croatian generals in Zagreb might not have passed down the direction to their troops

Lieutenant-Colonel Glenn Nordick on the War in Croatia

"As a Westerner, a Canadian, and a practicing Roman Catholic I had a great deal of difficulty understanding and accepting the depth of hatred and total disregard for human life that was prevalent among the leaders of both sides of this dispute at both the local and national levels. Violations of international law surrounded us (the ethnically cleansed villages, the mass graves, the systematically destroyed churches, and the ongoing and deliberate terrorizing and targeting of civilians)."

[top] Sergeant R.A. Dearing (without a helmet) with his section after the firefights at the Medak Pocket, Croatia, 1993. Dearing was awarded a Mention in Dispatches for valour under fire.

[bottom] Some key members of the orders group of 2 PPCLI, Medak Pocket, Croatia, 1993: [l to r] Regimental Sergeant Major, Chief Warrant Officer Mike McCarthy, Master Warrant Officer Mike Spellen, Major Dan Drew (in front of Spellen), Lieutenant-Colonel Jim Calvin, Commanding Officer, and Captain Wayne Eyre.

The initial deployment went smoothly, and by nine a.m. on September 15, C and D companies of the Patricias, the two French companies, the Anti-Armour Platoon, the Reconnaissance Platoon, and the combat engineers were all positioned around the town of Medak. That afternoon, however, when C Company, commanded by Major Brian Bailey, and one of the French companies moved between Serbian and Croatian forces, firefights broke out. As Calvin later reported, "On numerous occasions shortly after . . . Croatian forces directly engaged these UNPROFOR soldiers with small arms, heavy machine gun and in some instances 20mm cannon fire." Calvin's battle group returned fire that was obviously directed at them. Over the next fifteen hours, firefights, some lasting up to ninety minutes, continued with the Croats. Following the mission, both Sergeant Rod Dearing and Private Scotty Leblanc were awarded a Mention in Dispatches for

in the field that they were required to withdraw. Moreover, Canada earlier had decided to downsize its commitment to the Croatian theatre beginning with the next troop rotation, and in anticipation of the force reduction, both A Company and the Mortar Platoon had been ordered to leave their armoured personnel carriers and heavy weapons in Sector West when they deployed to Sector South. Just when Calvin needed all the firepower and protection he could get for his soldiers, he had lost his only indirect fire asset and one-quarter of his troop carriers. To help counter the lack of firepower, two French infantry companies were placed under Calvin's command.

[top] Ferreting out and impounding weapons caches was a routine task in peacekeeping operations in the Balkans.

[centre] A Patricia-occupied house, sandbagged and turned into a strongpoint, Croatia.

[bottom] Lipik, Croatia, one of the most devastated towns of the conflict at Medak Pocket.

leadership and valour under fire. That evening the Croats agreed to pull back the next day, and sporadic firefights continued until the morning. By first light on September 16, Phase One of the operation was largely complete: the Patricias had interposed themselves and stopped the fighting between Serbs and Croats.

The Patricias, however, were powerless to stop the atrocities within the Croatian-controlled area. At daybreak on September 16, they awoke "to the sounds of gunfire and explosions." Sergeant Jim Seggie described it: "[A]ll we could hear was explosions in the Medak Pocket. You could see the smoke rising and you knew darned well what was going on.... They're [the Croats] just blowing the houses up." But when Calvin sent in D Company, commanded by Major Dan Drew, to begin Phase Two and push into the buffer zone, as the ceasefire agreement of the previous night had provided for, Croatian troops backed by tanks stood in the Canadians' path. For an hour and a half, the

Canadians and the Croats faced off at ranges of fifty to a hundred metres. The Patricias had no tanks of their own but held each Croatian tank in the crosshairs of their anti-tank rocket launchers.

Determined to prevent needless bloodshed, Calvin called forward the numerous media crews accompanying his column and, in front of the Croatian troops, gave an interview in which he intentionally threatened the Croats' international reputation by claiming that Croatian soldiers were deliberately delaying the Canadian advance in order to hide evidence of "ethnic cleansing." On orders from their higher headquarters, the Croatian troops then relented, and as night fell the Patricias moved into the buffer zone and D Company occupied the Croatian front lines. Phase Two was complete. Yet, the Canadians' worst fears were realized. As Calvin later wrote, "The Croatians had systematically destroyed every building, poisoned every well, killed all the animals and purged the inhabitants. Sixteen bodies were found; some burned, some shot. Most bodies were civilian, both men and women. Highly suspicious were the surgical gloves littered on the ground…leading to the belief that even more individuals had been murdered, cleaned up, and transported out of the Pocket."

On September 17 and 18, the two French companies executed Phase Three of the operation and escorted the Croatian troops back to the September 9 start line. Tensions were high, and the Croats often resisted: on September 17, for example, the Patricias captured

and disarmed a sixteen-man fighting patrol that had entered the new buffer zone. The many minefields were especially dangerous: four French vehicles were lost to mines and seven French soldiers were badly wounded by mine explosions. Canadian Warrant Officer Bill Johnson was later awarded the Medal of Bravery for prodding through a Croatian minefield in the rain and darkness to rescue a French soldier who had been badly injured by an anti-personnel mine. On September 18, the Patricias suffered their only fatality of Medak: Captain Jim Decoste was killed when his jeep was struck by a Serbian Army truck redeploying troops from the area; two other Canadians, Lieutenant Rick Turner and Corporal Stacey Boake, were badly injured in the incident.

On September 19, Calvin's battle group began the final phase of the operation as Major Craig King and his sweep teams conducted a thorough search of the area to identify and remove bodies. Attached to King's group were a forensics team composed of UN officials, 2 PPCLI's doctor (Major Kelly Brett), and members of the Royal Canadian Mounted Police, charged to investigate war-crimes scenes. Warrant Officer Geoff Crossman commanded one such sweep team that was sent to a farm where it was reported two women had been burned: "We went to this area. It was the basement of a house. It was levelled but the basement was still there. I kicked the door in. There were 9mm rounds outside the door so we could only hope that they shot these two women before they burned them."

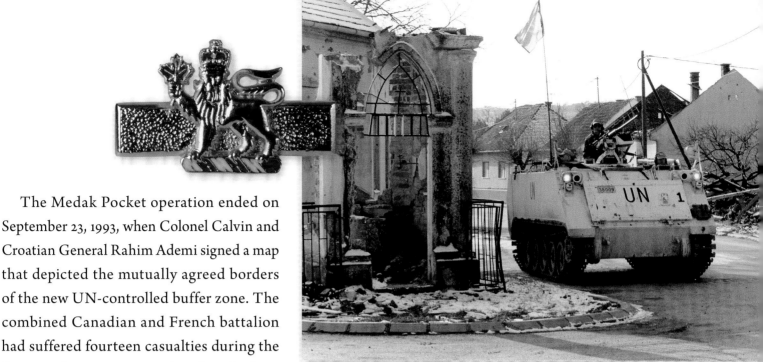

The Medak Pocket operation ended on September 23, 1993, when Colonel Calvin and Croatian General Rahim Ademi signed a map that depicted the mutually agreed borders of the new UN-controlled buffer zone. The combined Canadian and French battalion had suffered fourteen casualties during the fourteen-day mission: one Canadian dead, six Canadians wounded, seven French wounded. Croatian media reports indicated that as many as twenty-seven Croatian soldiers might have been killed. The battalion compiled a report on the ethnic cleansing that eventually resulted in war-crimes trials for both General Ademi and a Captain Noric; the former was acquitted, the latter sentenced to prison.

In Regimental history, the Medak Pocket was a relatively small operation, yet the Patricias' resolute stance signalled that Canada was prepared to meet force with force in this new and difficult environment. The Canadian government recognized that steadfastness by awarding the Meritorious Service Cross to Calvin and Mention in Dispatches to eight other members of the Patricias' battle group for their steadiness and bravery under fire during operations in the Medak Pocket. 2 PPCLI received the UNPROFOR force commander's Unit Commendation for turning back the Croatian attack on September 15 and successfully completing the mission despite fierce opposition. The battalion also received the Commander-in-Chief's Unit Commendation from Governor General

[left] Commander-in-Chief Unit Commendation. [RHK]

[right] An M113 armoured personnel carrier from 3 PPCLI patrols at Pakrac, Croatia.

Adrienne Clarkson. In the Medak Pocket, far from home, the Patricias came face to face with the realities of civil war and the knowledge that the nature of humanitarian intervention and traditional peacekeeping had changed. There was no peace to keep in the Balkans. That greater calamities had been averted was due to the understanding that, throughout the years of less-intensive peacekeeping, the Patricias and the Canadian Army never lost sight of the need for sustained hard training to keep sharp those battle skills that inevitably would be needed again. The years of diligent, focused effort in places such as Wainwright, Dundurn, Shilo, and Gagetown had proved their worth; when the need arose, the Patricias confirmed they were capable heirs to those who had soldiered before them.

In response to the growing ethnic turmoil in the former Yugoslavia, Canada, along with other

1 Section, 1 Platoon, A Company, 1 PPCLI, poses with local children while on patrol in the Glogovac region, Kosovo.

[top] 1 Platoon, A Company, 1 PPCLI, in front of the Ferro Nikel Plant, outside Glogovac, Kosovo, November 1999. The plant had been used as a base of operations by the Serbian Army and sustained significant damage during the NATO air campaign.

[facing page, top left] PPCLI mounts a Departure Guard for Lady Patricia, accompanied by the Commanding Officer, Lieutenant-Colonel Shane Brennan, Kosovo, October 26, 1999.

[facing page, bottom left] Lady Patricia and Major Stu Sharpe, Officer Commanding, A Company, 1 PPCLI, discuss the operation of a "visiting medical clinic" for locals with Ian Sumnall, Administrator, United Nations Interim Administration Mission in Kosovo, Gradicia, Kosovo, 1999.

[facing page, right] Lady Patricia and Major David Corbould, Officer Commanding, B Company, 1 PPCLI, on the main road west of the airport, Pristina, Kosovo, October 1999, with protection provided by the Anti-Armour Platoon and Lieutenant Bill Laidlaw.

[facing page, background] A field beside an old shirt factory was home for A Company for the first few days after its arrival in Kosovo, July 1999. Eventually, the main camp was set up inside the shirt factory and subsequently named Camp Spall.

member countries of the United Nations, deployed a peacekeeping force in an attempt to curb the violence and help stabilize the region, particularly in Bosnia-Herzegovina, Croatia, and Kosovo. The 1st, 2nd, and 3rd Battalions of the PPCLI were part of the Canadian Forces contribution to UNPROFOR.

The 1 PPCLI Battle Group arrived in Kosovo in early July 1999 to assume control of the Drenica area. By mid-August, the Patricias were in firm control of the region. ■

[top] A LAV III from C Company, 1 PPCLI, overtakes a horse and buggy along a road leading into Drvar, Bosnia, 2002. [CFJIC DND IS002-6672a]

[centre left] Soldiers of 1 PPCLI prepare to depart for Bosnia, 1994. Standing at attention is Sergeant Marc D. Leger, killed at Tarnak Farm, Afghanistan, eight years later. [CFJIC DND CLC94-48-4A]

[centre right] Lady Patricia presents medals to Patricias in Bosnia.

[bottom left] Lieutenant-Colonel Craig King, Commanding Officer, 1 PPCLI, on patrol in his LAV III near Crljeni, Bosnia, 2002. [CFJIC DND IS2002-6746a]

[facing page] Captain Kevin Schamuhn, A Company, 1 PPCLI, June 12, 2006. [CFJIC DND AR2006-A026-0095d]

[facing page, inset] NCM's Cap Badge 1956-present. [RHK]

[facing page, background] A Company patrol returns to Forward Operating Base Martello in the mountainous Wali Kot area, north of Kandahar, Afghanistan, May 13, 2006. [CFJIC DND AS2006-0437a]

2001-2013

[top] Corporals Ryan MacMillan and Chris Alden of 3 PPCLI wait before heading into a ravine to look for caves during Operation ANACONDA, Afghanistan, March 15, 2002. [CFJIC DND AP2002-5419]

[centre] Heavily weighted with ammunition, rations, water, and personal gear, soldiers of 3 PPCLI dismount from a US CH-47D Chinook helicopter, during Operation TOR II, Tora Bora region, Afghanistan, May 7, 2002. [CFJIC DND AP2002-5414]

[bottom] Lieutenant-Colonel Pat Stogran, Commanding Officer, 3 PPCLI, prepares for an air assault into the Gardez region, Afghanistan, March 13, 2002. [CFJIC DND AP2002-5237]

[background: CFJIC DND AS2006-0437a]

Afghanistan

The terrorist attacks of September 11, 2001, on New York City and Washington DC ushered in changing times for the Canadian Army. Although one hundred seventy Canadians had been killed on operational peacekeeping tours since the 1950s, and 2 PPCLI had actually fought a battle in the Medak Pocket in September 1993, no Canadian soldier had set out to fight a war since 1953 in Korea. That all changed in November 2001 when Prime Minister Jean Chrétien and Minister of National Defence Art Eggleton announced that Canada would send ground forces to Afghanistan to fight al-Qaeda, which had launched the attacks on the United States, and the Taliban, who had governed Afghanistan since 1996 and treated al-Qaeda as honoured guests. The mission would be carried out by a Canadian battle group formed around 3 PPCLI, augmented by a rifle company from 2 PPCLI and a squadron of Lord Strathcona's Horse (Royal Canadians) equipped with Coyote armoured reconnaissance vehicles, and with combat engineers in support. The battle group was commanded by Lieutenant-Colonel Patrick Stogran.

Few of Pat Stogran's soldiers were surprised by the announcement that they were heading for Afghanistan; they were Canada's NATO stand-by force, and NATO had resolved within days of 9/11 that the attack against the United States was deemed an attack against all the alliance. The Patricias quickly began full-scale training for the mission while the Canadian government searched for a suitable role for them. On

January 7, 2002, Defence Minister Eggleton held a press conference along with Chief of the Defence Staff General Ray Henault. His announcement stunned the nation: "After consulting with our allies and closely examining the military situation on the ground, we have decided to provide a battle group to support the US operation in the Kandahar area. The Canadian land force contingent will deploy to this area and will work with a United States combat team." The Patricias were to replace a battalion of the US 101st Airborne Division and serve under US operational command.

On Thursday, January 31, the first flight of troops bound for Kandahar left Edmonton aboard giant C-5 transports of the United States Air Force. They flew to Frankfurt-am-Main, Germany, where they transferred to large C-17s for the long flight to Afghanistan. The first plane landed two days later at Kandahar Airfield at four-thirty a.m. local time in near-freezing weather. One of the first Coyotes unloaded bore the painted words "I love New York" on its rear door.

Stogran, who had arrived several days earlier, was in his bunk when the first plane landed. He gathered the seventy soldiers from the first two aircraft to remind them that this mission was unlike any they had ever undertaken and to warn them to be very careful. As usual, Stogran minced no words and, also as usual, his soldiers appreciated his straightforward attitude: "He's a tough man — aggressive but thoughtful, considerate and deliberate in his decisions," Sergeant Mike Gauley told a reporter. "He's the right man to lead us."

On February 11, the Canadian flag was formally raised at the base; by then, more than two-thirds of the Canadians had set up shop. At first, Strathcona Coyotes patrolled the base perimeter within the outer defensive wire, but as the Canadian battle group went operational by mid-month, they began to venture beyond the wire to help reconnoitre possible approaches to the base. The Patricias mostly used US-made Humvees (Hummers) for infantry patrol duty. Lightly armoured and mounting heavy machine guns, they were ideal for covering ground in the bleak, high desert country. When not on patrol or a combat mission, the soldiers began their day by arising from their canvas cots for a morning run. There were no huts — just tents and rations and water that had been run through so many purification procedures that it was "stripped of its natural goodness." There was almost no electricity, and outhouses and latrines dotted the base. As winter ended, the days grew hotter and fine sand sifted into everything.

The Patricias first went into action at the end of February in Operation ANACONDA, an American-led attack to clear a mountainous and cave-ridden area near Gardez, about one hundred fifty kilometres south of Kabul. Coalition forces from six countries were involved, alongside some fifteen hundred local Afghan fighters. In the first part of the operation, six Patricia snipers accompanied troops of two separate battalions of the 101st Airborne, which advanced under fire along a series of ridge lines as US B-52s

Welcome to Kandahar

CBC Radio reporter Mike Smith, a former member of the PPCLI and Canadian Airborne Regiment, arrived at the Kandahar base in late March to cover the story. He described the countryside this way: "There is nothing. It is where water goes to die; a plant's concept of hell. Baked-hard mud littered with rocks is the only flora here. Beetles and snakes the only daytime fauna." Every day began and ended the same way, with the mornings "bright and crisp, not a cloud in the sky and the temperature around eight degrees...the nights...just as spectacular as the mornings — cool breezes under a blanket of stars."

Soldiers of 9 Platoon, C Company, 1 PPCLI, on patrol near Forward Operating Base Robinson, Afghanistan, April 17, 2006.

wheeled high over the Shah-e-Kot mountain range dropping precision-guided munitions into caves and defiles. On Wednesday, March 13, the largest number of Patricias involved so far in the campaign took part in Operation HARPOON, under Stogran's command, to clear the area south of Gardez. Five hundred Patricias and one hundred Americans began the assault, airlifted into the mountainous region by large US Chinook helicopters from an airbase at Bagram, fifty-five minutes away. The troops had been told that between sixty and eighty al-Qaeda fighters were holed

[top] Warrant Officer Shaun Peterson escorts the bodies of Sergeant Vaughan Ingram, corporals Chris Reid and Bryce Keller, and Private Kevin Dallaire during a Ramp Ceremony at Kandahar Airfield, August 5, 2006. [CFJIC DND AR2006-A042-0015d]

[bottom] Soldiers of 3 PPCLI and the US 101st Airborne Division build C-4 explosive charges before destroying caves during Operation TOR II, Tora Bora region, May 7, 2002. [CFJIC DND AP2002-5424]

[facing page centre] Patrolling and maintaining a presence among the people of Afghanistan was as important a task as bringing the fight to the enemy in his strongholds. [CFJIC DND AR2005-A01-103a]

[facing page bottom] Major Bill Fletcher, Officer Commanding C Company, 1 PPCLI, conducts a meeting with village elders from Garmak, west of Kandahar, April 2, 2006. [CFJIC DND AS2006-0321a]

Sergeant A.K. (Austin) Williams, Corporal Hipkin, and another soldier from 9 Platoon, C Company, 1 PPCLI, on patrol in the Sangin district, Afghanistan, April 2006. [CFJIC DND KA2006-R106-0141d]

[left] Governor General Adrienne Clarkson speaks with Corporal William McCulligh as she reviews an Honour Guard from Operation ATHENA at Camp Julien, Kabul, Afghanistan, December 3, 2003. [CFJIC DND KA2003-A472A]

[centre] Members of 3 PPCLI trek through rugged terrain during Operation CHEROKEE SKY, Afghanistan, July 4, 2002. [CFJIC DND IS2002-2114]

[bottom] Patricias of C Company, 1 PPCLI, at Forward Operating Base Robinson. sleep beside their LAV III after a long night move, Afghanistan, summer 2006. Living out of the LAV was as good as it got for many Patricias of Task Force Orion. [CFJIC DND As2006-0295a]

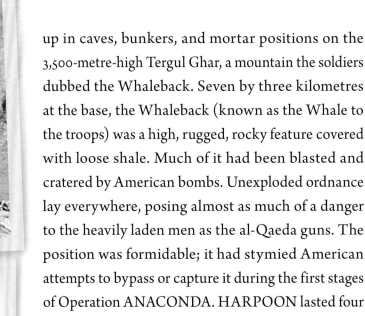

up in caves, bunkers, and mortar positions on the 3,500-metre-high Tergul Ghar, a mountain the soldiers dubbed the Whaleback. Seven by three kilometres at the base, the Whaleback (known as the Whale to the troops) was a high, rugged, rocky feature covered with loose shale. Much of it had been blasted and cratered by American bombs. Unexploded ordnance lay everywhere, posing almost as much of a danger to the heavily laden men as the al-Qaeda guns. The position was formidable; it had stymied American attempts to bypass or capture it during the first stages of Operation ANACONDA. HARPOON lasted four days, but luckily the only Canadian casualties were broken bones and sprained ankles; most of the enemy had evacuated their positions.

The first Canadians killed in Afghanistan, in fact, were victims of friendly fire: four Patricias who were inadvertently attacked in the early morning hours of April 18, 2002, by two US Air Force fighter bombers. The Patricias had been conducting a night exercise at a training area named Tarnak Farm some fifteen

Members of 3 PPCLI march through the dust to an after-action briefing on Operation ANACONDA, Bagram Air Base, March 19, 2002. [CFJIC DND AP2002-5212]

Ian Hope on the Challenges Commanders Faced in Afghanistan

"The moral authority of the commanders, not their rank or appointment, was essential in this fighting, and the moral judgment of commanders and their personal example were required every minute to keep our troops moving forward in places fraught with danger."

kilometres south of their base at the Kandahar Airfield. One of the US pilots saw tracer fire used during the exercise and somehow mistook it for enemy fire directed at his fighter. The pilot mistakenly dropped a laser-guided bomb and four Patricias were killed. It was a tremendous shock to Canadians at home who only then began to wake up to the fact that Canadian soldiers had been sent to fight a war in a mysterious and faraway country about which most Canadians knew nothing.

The Patricia battle group left Afghanistan in the summer of 2002; Canada stayed out of Afghanistan until late summer 2003, when Ottawa sent troops to lead the International Security Assistance Force (ISAF), a new NATO mission to keep the peace, first in Kabul and then in most of the rest of Afghanistan. As part of the new mission, the United States would end its Operation Enduring Freedom in Kandahar Province in July 2006 and hand over security operations for the province to the Canadians. Accordingly, in August 2005, the Canadians closed their base in Kabul and moved south to Kandahar Airfield to prepare to take over from the Americans. The Canadians' aim was to set up and

operate a Provincial Reconstruction Team (PRT) in the northern outskirts of Kandahar City, train Afghan National Security Forces in the region, and provide the military security necessary to protect the PRT and to allow civil government to be reconstructed in that vital province. 3 PPCLI provided the first PRT, based just north of Kandahar at Camp Nathan Smith, named after one of the Canadian soldiers who had been killed at Tarnak Farm.

[top] A dust storm at Forward Operating Base Robinson drives soldiers of C Company, 1 PPCLI, to take cover in their LAV III, April 1, 2006. [CFJIC DND AS2006-0303a]

[bottom] Patricias from 1 PPCLI take a brief operational pause while crossing a wide expanse of terrain, Kandahar, summer 2006. [PPCLI RHQ]

The first battle group, Task Force Orion, was based on 1 PPCLI, commanded by Lieutenant-Colonel Ian Hope, who borrowed a page from Big Jim Stone's Korea Regimental history. Unsatisfied with his men's pre-deployment training in Canada, Hope kept them out of the fight until he felt their combat-readiness training was complete. When the task force assumed control of the province in February 2006, it made contact with the Taliban almost immediately. Between February and May, the Patricias scoured northern and western Kandahar Province to search out enemy

sanctuaries, occasionally encountering armed groups and suffering casualties from improvised explosive devices.

Serious fighting broke out in neighbouring Helmand Province on March 29, 2006, and Patricias were deployed there for five weeks to pacify the area in advance of the arrival of the 3rd Battalion of the British Army's Parachute Regiment. This period of short, brutal, isolated firefights and ambushes saw the first Patricias killed in action in Afghanistan. In April the tempo of operations increased as the Taliban attempted to establish permanent bases to the west of Kandahar City from which to launch high-profile attacks. Hundreds of fighters surged into the province from Pakistan, and the Patricias began a long series of offensive operations to find and disrupt Taliban groups. Between early May and late August, Task Force Orion conducted eighteen offensive operations, making contact with massed Taliban fighters on all but two occasions. Making maximum use of intelligence, surveillance, and reconnaissance assets, as well as artillery fire and ground manoeuvre using elaborate

Captain Slade Lerch, 3 PPCLI Task Force 1-08, Operational Mentoring and Liaison Team, watches for enemy activity across the Arghandab River, Panjwayi district, August 8, 2008. [PPCLI RHQ]

deception, the Patricias successfully executed multiple night operations to destroy Taliban groups. In all there were more than fifty sizable engagements involving the movement of multiple company groups, M777 155mm howitzer fire, armed and unarmed unmanned aerial vehicles (UAVs), multiple electronic warfare platforms, Apache helicopter gunship fire, close air support from A-10 Warthogs, fast air support, and precision-guided munitions from B1 bombers. The Patricias lived in and fought from their Light Armoured Vehicles for weeks without stop, gaining only periodic and short recesses in Kandahar Airfield. The area of operations expanded steadily to incorporate all of northern Kandahar Province and, for three weeks in July, most of northern Helmand Province, which was two hundred kilometres from the PPCLI supply base.

Task Force Orion's efforts killed and captured more than five hundred of the enemy, prevented Taliban attacks in Kandahar City, and set the conditions for deployments of British and Dutch troops into southern Afghanistan and the subsequent transfer of the area of operations to NATO/ISAF. The cost to the battle group, though, was 10 per cent casualties. After its return to Canada, 1 PPCLI was given the Commander-in-Chief's Unit Commendation by the Governor General for "exceptional determination and courage during relentless combat in Afghanistan" in what was the Regiment's heaviest episode of sustained fighting since Korea.

Patricias from the 3rd Battalion returned to Kandahar in 2007, supplying soldiers and leaders for newly formed Operational Mentoring and Liaison teams (OMLT) operating in small groups alongside Afghan National Army soldiers in Kandahar and Helmand. When Canada shifted its efforts from combat to combat training operations in 2011, 3 PPCLI also took on the bulk of training and mentoring functions at numerous Afghan National Army training centres in Kabul. Between February and August 2008, 2 PPCLI deployed to continue ISAF operations in southern Afghanistan and, in a pioneering use of UAVs, conducted more than ninety missile strikes, killing hundreds of Taliban insurgents. The 1st Battalion deployed again to Kandahar from August 2009 to March 2010, conducting aggressive counterinsurgency operations that completely dominated the contended Zhari and Panjwayi districts and overseeing the reintroduction of US ground forces into the area of operations.

[top] 2 Platoon, A Company, working in tandem with their LAV III. The small black caps on the ground are empty casings from an M-203 grenade launcher. [SK]

[centre right] Sergeant Chuck Prodonik, 2 Platoon, A Company, 1 PPCLI, during a firefight in the Panjwayi district, July 2006. In the foreground lies an M-72 light anti-tank weapon, which has been fired. [SK]

[bottom left] A rifleman of 1 PPCLI Battle Group with the ubiquitous M-72 light anti-tank weapon during a firefight in the Panjwayi district. [SK]

[background: CFJIC DND AS2006-0437a]

[top] Patricias try to identify Taliban insurgents during operations in Kandahar Province. [SK]

[left] Troops from 9 Platoon, C Company, 1 PPCLI, clear a hut during combat operations, Afghanistan, 2006. [CFJIC DND]

[bottom] Private K.C. (Kevin) Slack, A Company, 1 PPCLI, suppresses the enemy with his C-6 general purpose machine gun. [SK]

The work of the PPCLI battalions in Afghanistan ever since the introduction of Canadian troops in January 2002 has demonstrated once again the Patricias' incredible versatility, resilience, and fighting tenacity. Since the end of Canada's mission in Kandahar Province in late summer 2011, the remaining Patricias in Afghanistan are focused until 2014 on training members of the Afghan National Army, mainly in Kabul. As Canada's commitment to Afghanistan winds down, Patricia's can take pride in the fact that with courage, skill, and resolve they successfully and professionally completed their assigned tasks.

The history of the Patricias, one hundred years after it began, sees the nation at peace and the Regiment focused on training and honing its fighting skills. No doubt, Canada will again feel it necessary to deploy troops to dangerous and troubled parts of the world. When it does, the PPCLI will be ready. The Patricia heritage is one of character, skill, valour, and loyalty. If the light of the past can in any way illuminate the path of the future, Canada can be assured that the Patricias will once again uphold the standards they have come to exemplify. ∎

The Memorial Hall of Honour Dedicated to the Memory of Patricias who gave their lives in service to Canada

The central area of the Regimental Museum, located within the Military Museums of Calgary, encompasses the "Memorial Hall of Honour" where the names of all the fallen Patricias are etched in wall-mounted granite tablets.

The Memorial Hall also houses an original portrait of the young Princess Patricia and the original Camp Colour (the "Ric-A-Dam-Doo"), hand-stitched by Princess Patricia and carried into battle by the Regiment during the First World War. [RHK]

WW I

PTE W READ
PTE E READING
PTE EC REED
PTE H REEKIE
PTE D REES
PTE T REGAN
PTE EJ REID
PTE SJ REID
PTE W REID
PTE J RENNIE
PTE DB RENNOLDSON
PTE JG REYMOND
PTE HA RIACH
PTE AS RICHARDS
PTE CA RICHARDS
PTE JS RICHARDS
L/CPL CD RICHARDSON
PTE D RICHARDSON
A/CPL GA RICHARDSON
PTE ER RICHES
LT JR RIDDELL
SGT SJ RIDLEY MM
PTE DT RIEKIE
PTE T RIGG
PTE T RITCHIE
SGT HW RITTENHOUSE
PTE CJW RITTER
PTE W ROACH
PTE J ROBERTS
PTE JG ROBERTS
SGT JLA ROBERTSON
PTE R ROBERTSON
PTE SG ROBERTSON
PTE WM ROBERTSON
PTE WT ROBERTSON
LT AJ ROBINS
PTE AEF ROBINSON
PTE C ROBINSON
PTE J ROBINSON
PTE MA ROBINSON
L/CPL P ROBSON
PTE FR ROCK
PTE MT ROETT
PTE E ROPER
LT AG ROSAMOND
L/CPL JH ROSHER
CPL D ROSS
PTE H ROSS
PTE J ROSS
PTE E ROSSITER
PTE J ROTHSCHILD
L/CPL DS ROUGH
PTE J ROUTLEDGE
PTE JA ROWE
PTE J ROWLEY
PTE WM ROYS
SGT T RUDDIGAN
PTE WL RUDDY
PTE J RUSSELL
PTE S RUSTON
PTE WF RYAN
PTE W SABEAN
PTE L SALSBURY
PTE W SAVELL
SGT MD SCHELL DCM
PTE D SCOTT
PTE J SCOTT
PTE J SCOTT
PTE JA SCOTT
PTE JJ SCOTT
PTE JW SCOTTING
PTE WH SCREEN
PTE G SEGUIN
PTE G SELLEY
PTE R SERO
SGT JF SEXTON
PTE DC SEYMOUR
PTE O SHARP

WW I

PTE RW SHAR
PTE AJ SHAVE
PTE HS SHAVE
PTE H SHAW
PTE HR SHEAR
PTE JD SHEAR
PTE G SHEPHE
PTE AJ SHEPPA
PTE G SHEPPA
PTE L SHERRI
L/CPL JC SHIP
PTE AH SHUTE
PTE HRS SHUT
PTE RE SHUTTLEWO
PTE CJ SIBARY
PTE E SILCOX
PTE T SILLENO
PTE GR SILSON
PTE GB SIMMO
LT RH SIMOND
PTE PA SIMON
PTE H SIMPSO
PTE PM SIMPS
PTE R SIMPSO
PTE AJ SINCLA
PTE C SINGER
L/CPL HA SKE
LT RL SLADEN
PTE B SLATER
PTE JP SLOAN
PTE J SLONEM
PTE AG SMALL
PTE W SMEDL
PTE A SMITH
PTE C SMITH
PTE C SMITH
PTE CK SMITH
PTE EJ SMITH
PTE H SMITH
CSM HGL SMIT
SGT J SMITH
PTE JA SMITH
PTE LR SMITH
PTE R SMITH
PTE R SMITH
PTE FG SNARE
PTE FJ SNIDE
PTE RD SNOW
PTE CW SNYD
PTE WE SOLLA
L/CPL W SOW
SGT R SPALL V
PTE J SPANSW
PTE AJ SPARK
PTE A SPLICER
PTE TA SPOOR
PTE E ST AMO
SGT W STANBOROU
PTE RA STANB
PTE FW STANI
PTE RR STAVE
L/CPL GW STA
PTE JH STEEL
PTE JE STEND
PTE A STEPHE
PTE WJ STEPH
PTE SS STEIN
PTE J STEVEN
PTE AE STEVE
L/SGT AW STE
L/CPL O STEV
LT COL CJT STEWAR
PTE EM STEWA
L/CPL GB STEW
LT J STEWART
PTE J STEWAR
PTE W STEWA
CPL AT STONE

DEDICATED TO THE MEMORY OF
ALL PATRICIAS WHO GAVE
THEIR LIVES IN THE CAUSE OF
PEACE, FREEDOM AND JUSTICE

Image Credits

All images are reproduced courtesy of the Princess Patricia's Canadian Light Infantry Museum and Archives unless otherwise note below.

Images of badges and crests on the title page and on pages 23, 24, 33, 43, 49, 52, 57, 70, 73, 77, 86, 89, 90, 96, 99, 105, 115, 119, and 133 [RHK] are reproduced courtesy of the Princess Patricia's Canadian Light Infantry Museum and Archives/Ryan HK Photography|Motion, Calgary.

Images on pages 8, 9, 31, 128, and 129 [PPCLI RHQ] are reproduced courtesy of the Princess Patricia's Canadian Light Infantry Regimental Headquarters.

Images on pages 33, 44, 52, 63, 65, 66, 71, 78, 80, 82, 83, and 93 [LAC/DND] are reproduced courtesy of Library and Archives Canada/Department of National Defence Fonds.

Images on pages 73, 74, 80, 85, 89, 90, 101, 102, 103, 104, 105, 108, 109, 118, 119, 120, 124, 125, 126, 127, 128, 130, 131, and the back cover [CFJIC DND] are reproduced courtesy of Canadian Forces Joint Imaging Centre of the Department of National Defence.

Images pages 130 and 131 [SK] are reproduced courtesy of Scott Kesterson, Documentary Filmmaker, Panjwai 2006. Copyright © 2013 by Scott Kesterson.

Images on pages 54 and 55 [GW] are reproduced courtesy of George Wilkinson, Victoria, B.C.

The image on page 23 [CVA] is reproduced courtesy of City of Vancouver Archives.

The image of Sergeant Robert Spall, VC, on page 43 [Canadian War Museum 19910109-743] is from the George Metcalf Archival Collection copyright © by the Canadian War Museum and reproduced courtesy of the Canadian War Museum.

The reproduction of the painting on page 68, Charles Comfort (British, 1900-1994), *The Hitler Line*, 1944, oil on canvas, 101.6 x 121.7 cm, Beaverbrook Collection of War Art, [Canadian War Museum 19710261-2203], is reproduced courtesy of the Canadian War Museum.

Index